Oxford New Geography 2

a course for juniors

Gordon Elliott

Contents

Oxford University Press

The street

The hawk is a hunting bird. It has very good eyesight. It uses its eyes to spot its food. It is always alert.

Hawk's eye view of the countryside

Hawk's eye view of a town

Are you alert? Do you notice things which other people miss? Start with the picture below. There are ten deliberate mistakes. What are they? Make a list of them.

John has been practising **eye-spy**. He drew five things he could see above him. Then he drew five things he saw at eye level and five objects he saw when he looked down.

These are some of the things he saw by looking up.

A window

The top of a door

These are some objects he saw at eye level.

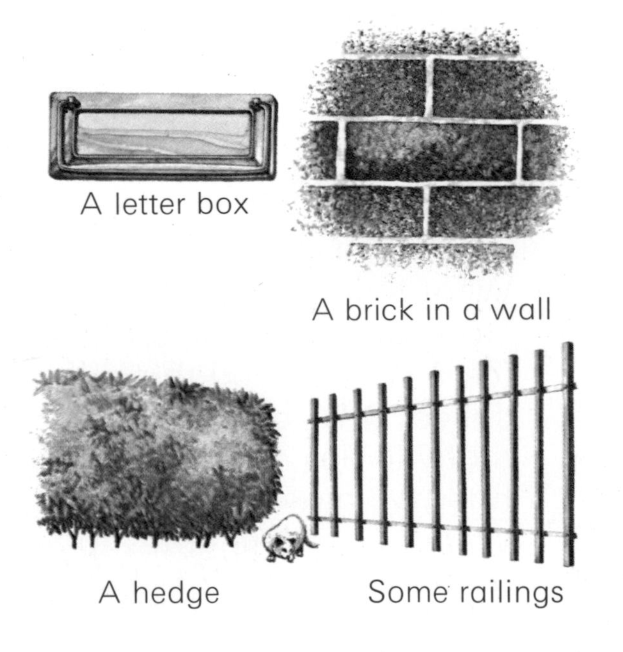

A letter box

A brick in a wall

A hedge

Some railings

These are some of the things he saw when he looked down.

A drain

A paving stone

A gutter with a drain

John made fifteen drawings and labelled each one. When he had to look up to find something he put an arrow next to the object. It pointed upwards. ↑

He also drew these arrows next to some objects.

→

What did they mean?

Look around your own school or street. Make fifteen drawings of things you see. Write a label next to each one and put an arrow beside it like John did.

Danger Note

Streets can be dangerous places. Take care. Keep on the pavement. Don't cross the road unless you check that it is clear. Don't do eye-spy work when it is getting dark.

Counting traffic

John's school is in Hawk Street. His mother tells him to take care on the way to school because the roads are busy. Look at the picture of Hawk Street. Write some sentences about it.

How they did it

John and his friend are counting traffic. They are outside the school gates and are standing near the wall. This means they are at a safe distance from the road. They are not in the way of people walking past. They have sheets of paper clipped to a piece of hardboard. They use this for their answers.

Each time a car went past they put a | on the paper in the space marked **cars.** When a lorry went past they put a | in the space marked **lorries.** They also had a space for **vans.**

How many cars had they seen when they had written 𝍸? They did it this way so they could count up their totals in fives.

Start 11·00	Finish 11·30	Total
Cars	𝍸 𝍸 𝍸 𝍸 𝍸 ||	27
Lorries	𝍸 𝍸 |||	
Vans	𝍸 𝍸 𝍸 𝍸 |	
Others	𝍸	

Make a copy of the chart and fill in the totals. Then write answers to these questions. In which space would they put a | if a bicycle went past? How many lorries did they see? What time did they start? What time did they finish? How long did their survey last? Why do you think John called 𝍸 a gate? How many lorries had he seen if he had two gates on his sheet? Were there more gates for cars than lorries in John's survey?

John's class wanted to know if streets in other areas were like Hawk Street. They asked their teacher. Mr. Brown said he did not know but he would write to another school to find out. He wrote to a teacher in Wales.

West Midlands Education Committee
Brington Primary School,
Hawk Street, Bradley, West Midlands CV32 6AT.
Telephone: 0203 67912

29 May 1980

Dear Mr. Thomas,

We are counting traffic in the street outside our school. The children asked if two pupils would do a count of traffic outside your school between eleven and half past eleven on a weekday morning, and send us the results. Thank you for your help.

Yours sincerely,

Jeremy Brown

Mr. Thomas asked his class to do a traffic count. Use the picture to write answers to these questions. What time did they do the survey? How long did it last? Why did they choose this time? (**Clue** – check what time John did his survey.)

		Total
Cars	𝍸 𝍸 𝍸	
Lorries	|||	
Vans	||||	
Others	𝍸	

These are the results from the Welsh school. Make a copy of the chart. Fill in the totals. Give the chart a title.

The two charts below were made by John's class. They used the numbers from the two surveys to make them.

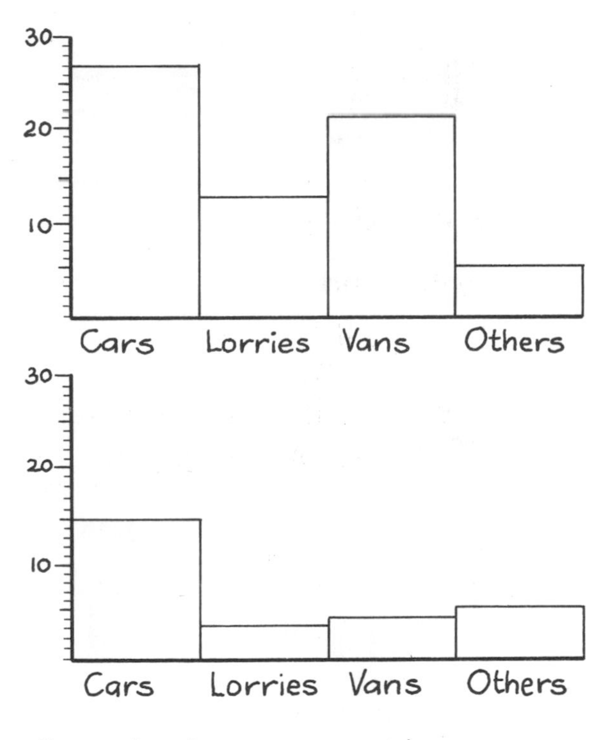

Cars, lorries, vans and bicycles are all vehicles.

Now write answers to these questions. How many vehicles went along Hawk Street? How many vehicles were counted by the Welsh children? Which street had more? Which is the busier street? Are streets in towns usually busier than roads in the country?

Focus on traffic

Here are eight traffic pictures. Their labels have been mixed up. Copy the numbers. Find the right label for each picture and write it next to the number. Number 4 should be **taxi.** What are the rest?

Now try these.

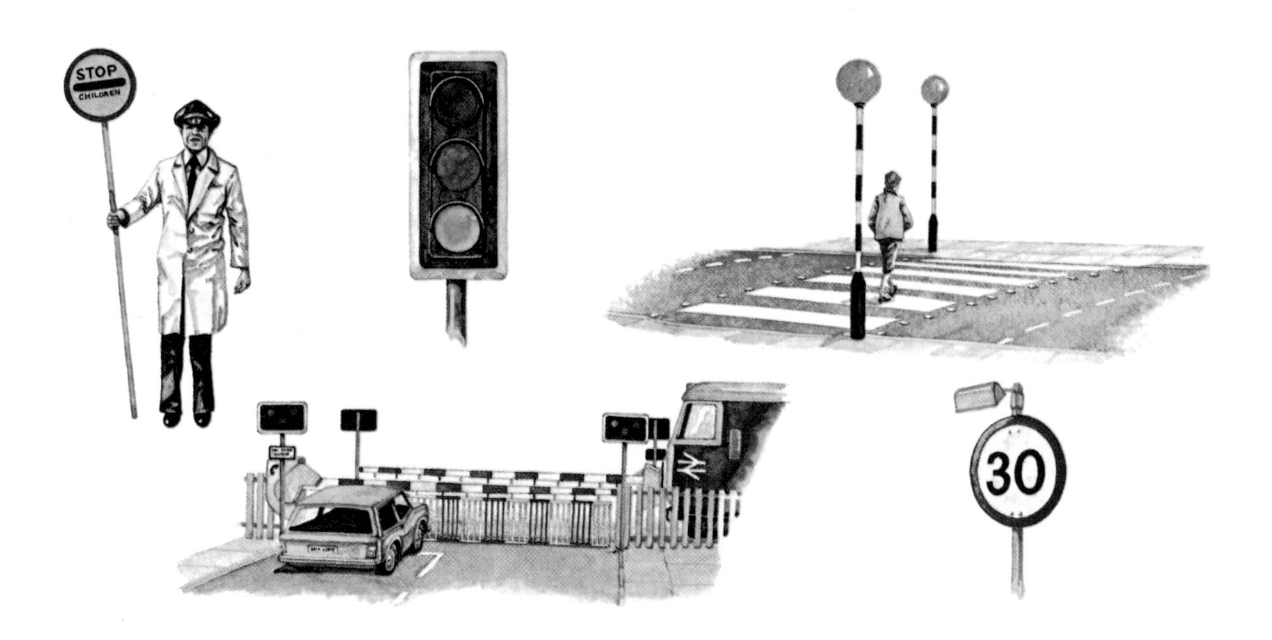

Make a quiz

For this you will first need to collect ten traffic pictures from newspapers and magazines. You can then test your friends. Show them one of the pictures. They have to say what it is and write down the answer. If they get an answer wrong they lose a mark.

This is a picture of the High Street. Each day a lot of traffic goes past the school. It is not so busy now. It is busiest when the children are going to and from school.

Because there is a lot of traffic the council has decided to put a zebra crossing on the street. It will help the children. They will be able to cross the busy road more easily.

If you were the council, where would you put the zebra crossing? Would it be a good idea to put it right next to the crossroads, or very close to the bus stops? Could the bus stops be moved?

Talk about it with your friends. Do you agree where the best place is? What does the rest of the class think?

Checking

Thinking

This is one of the pictures you saw on page 2.

This is a plan of the church, farm and fields you can see in the picture.

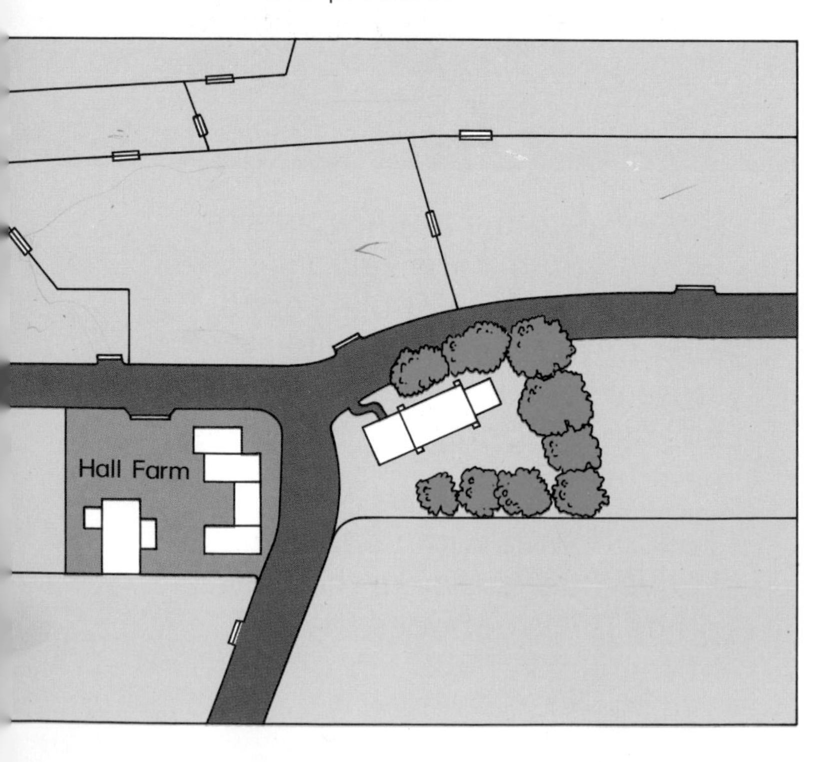

Make two headings.

1 Things I can see in the picture.
2 Things I can see on the plan.

Use the picture and plan to make lists of words under each heading.

A walk

John and his friend are on holiday at Hall Farm. They want to go for a walk. It has been raining. They cannot go across ploughed fields as they would get too muddy. They have to walk round the edges. But they can walk across the grass fields.

They go through the gate opposite the farm and into the grass field. They cross this field to the gate and go into the next grass field.

They want to go into three other fields before they get back to the road. Look at the picture and find which way they go.

Then make a copy of the plan on a piece of paper. Draw a line on it to show the way they go.

Doing

Some streets are noisy. Some are quiet. Make a list of the names of streets near your school. Which are noisy? Which are quiet?

These are three noisy vehicles. What noises do they make? Why are they noisy?

Puzzle corner

What is it? Where is it?

You could make puzzles like this. Collect pictures of things. They may be famous buildings or people. They may be things that are well known in your town or village. When you have collected them, write a question for each one.

Going further

On your way to school make a note of the noises you can hear in the street and what makes them. Then make a list of them. Here are three to start you off.

Object	Noise
motor bike	roar
children	chatter
bell	clang

Eye-spy

Have you played eye-spy? **I spy with my little eye something beginning with A . . .** You then try to guess what the object is. If you get it right, it is your turn to say **I spy with my little eye . . .**

Hawk eye

This sign shows that its owner belongs to a football club. Make a sign for a **hawk eye** badge. The badge could be given to the best hawk eye in your class.

Then and now

Look carefully at the two large pictures. The picture on page 11 shows part of a town in 1900. The picture on this page shows what it is like today.

This is Rachel. She lives in a flat above one of the shops. Her grandmother lives nearby.

Rachel is going to the shops with her grandmother who is eighty years old. You can see them in the picture. They are near the dairy. They have to be careful when they cross High Street. It is a busy road with many shops and a lot of traffic.

Rachel – aged 8

Grandma Adelaide – aged 80

1900 was a long time ago. On this page you will see a picture of Grandma Adelaide in 1900. She was only a baby then.

You can see her pram outside the dairy in the large picture.

Baby Adelaide – aged 6 months

If you look carefully at the two pictures you will see that some things have changed between 1900 and today. Look at the ten numbers on each picture. Number **1** on today's picture shows a garden. In 1900 this was a field where a farmer kept his cows. If you look carefully you will also see that part of the field is now a road.

Make a list of the numbers. Write a sentence saying what each number is today. Then write what it was like in 1900. Put a tick next to the things that have changed.

Clues from the past

How do we know what places were like a long time ago? Old photographs can help. Look at this one which shows a street in 1900. The street was in a town. There were shops but they were different from those we know today. Can you see how different they were? You will also notice that clothes were different then.

We can sometimes learn what streets were like from old plans. This one shows part of a street in 1900.

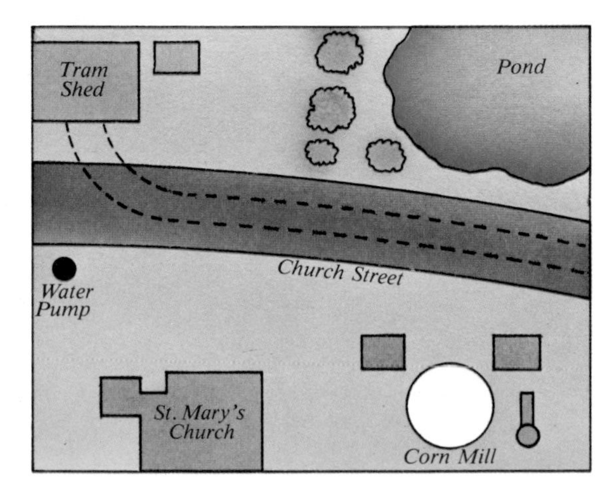

There were trams in those days. They ran along rails in the street. People rode on them to get to work or go shopping.

There was a water pump in this street. It was used for pumping water into a big trough. Horses could get a drink there. The horses were used for pulling carts.

Here is a picture of a corn mill. Find it on the plan. It was knocked down twenty years ago.

Rachel is talking to her grandmother. She is asking her what the town was like when she was young. Her grandmother can remember riding on a tram. They were used to carry people before buses were common. At first trams were pulled by horses. Then they were driven by electricity.

Talking to old people

Your grandparents and other old people may be able to tell you what places were like when they were young.

This is a page in an old book that Paul takes to school. It is over seventy years old and belongs to his father.

Haines Miss, London street
Hands James Bell, Gloucester street
Hawkes Frederick Arthur, Westbrook villas, Gravel walk
Heavens William Carter, Hillfarm house, Stanford road
Hey Harold Darwin, Eastfield
Hodgson Rev. Arthur Charles [Baptist], Westbrook villa, Bromsgrove place
Howse Miss, 3 Westfield villas
James Mrs. Astley house

Part of a street directory

Paul is interested because he lives in an old house. The house is listed in the book with all the others in the town. He finds that William Carter Heavens used to live there. What was his address?

Paul is able to check the age of his house. The builder had fixed a date stone in the wall. It gives the date when the house was built. Not every house has one.

A date stone on a house

Have you seen any houses with date stones? What is the oldest house you know? Find out when it was built.

Looking at plans

This is a modern plan of the area where Rachel lives. It is shown in the picture on page 10.

Plans show what things would look like from above. If you looked straight down on the shops and houses, these are the shapes they would be. Not everything is shown on the plan. For example, people and traffic are not shown.

First look at the picture on page 10. Now look at the plan. Answer these questions.

1 What is building **A**?
2 What shops are on each side of **B**?
3 What is **C** on the picture?
4 What is there at **D**?
5 What do the initials **P.O.** and **P.H.** mean?
6 Rachel lives in a flat above Hill's shop. Which letter on the plan shows where the flat is?

This is an old plan of the area where Rachel lives. It was made in 1900.

What was building **A** in 1900? How many houses have been made into shops between 1900 and today? Name three things that are on today's plan but not 1900's.

Look at the plan for 1900. Sort out the numbers to fit the correct label.

A field
Market Cross
Dairy
The Grapes
The place where the horse drawn bus would be
The place where there is a gate into a field
A wood
A gas lamp

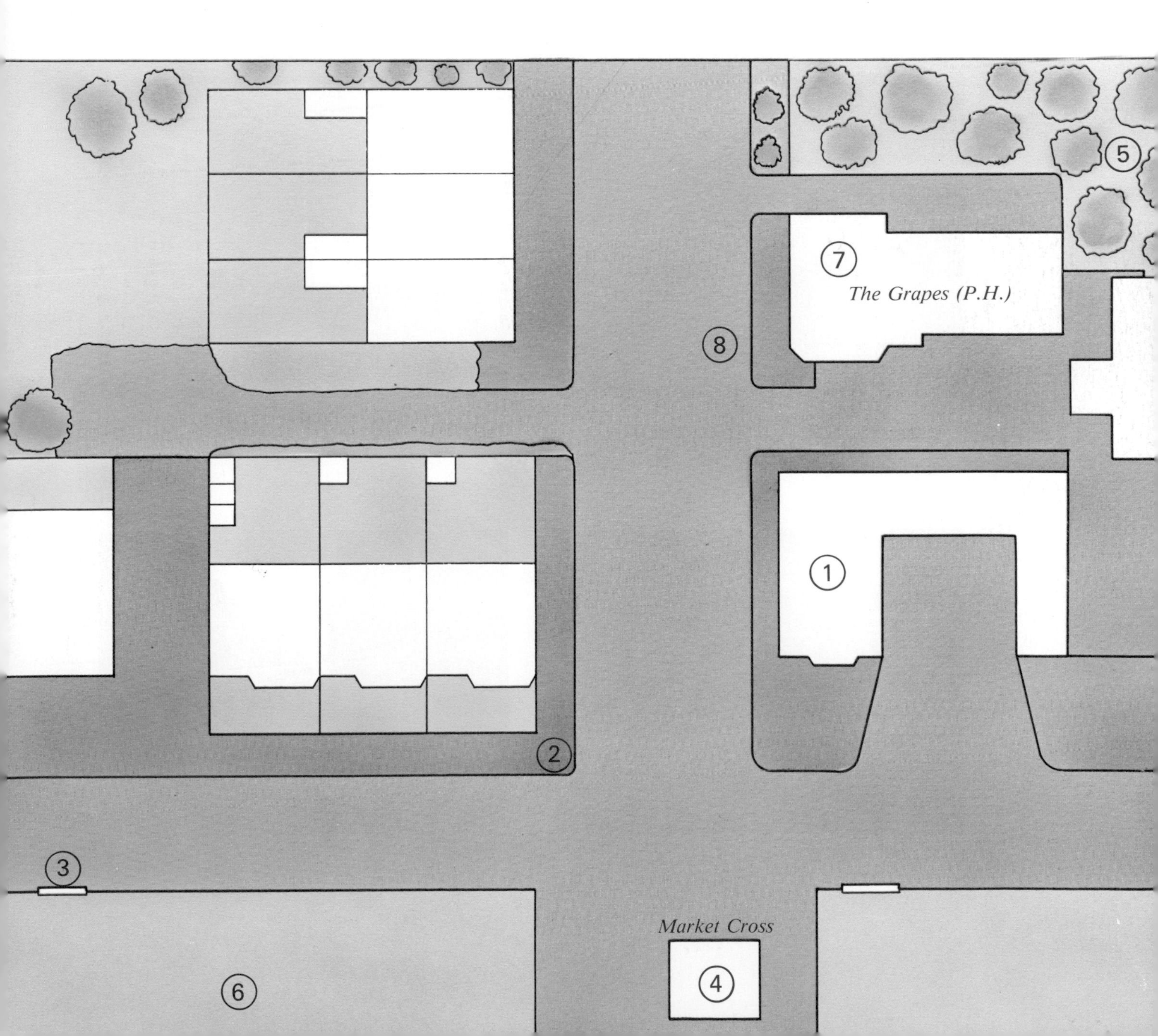

Checking

Thinking

Write the answers to the questions.

Which is the old street? Which is the new? How can you tell?

If you wanted to go shopping, which street would you go to?
What kinds of things could you buy?

Which is the village street? Where would the other one be?

Doing

Try making a model like this.

First, put a large sheet of paper on the table. Get some building blocks or old boxes.

Set them out on the paper. Imagine they are buildings in a street.

Draw around each block or box. Then take it away. You are left with a plan of the block. What shape is it?

These are shapes.

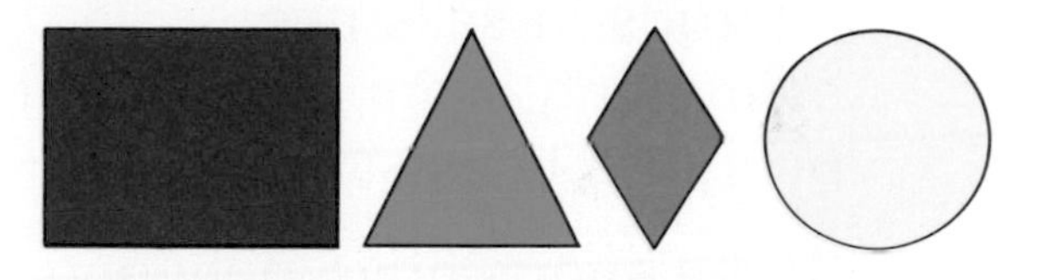

What shapes are they? Which shape would fit most of the buildings you know?

Spotting shapes

Who or what is this?

Answer: It is a Mexican frying an egg. You are looking at him from above. Mexicans often wear big hats called sombreros.

Shops

Shops can be large. Some are small.

They can be on their own. Some are found with others in a group. We call this a cluster of shops.

Shops might only sell one kind of thing. For example, a fish shop usually sells just fish. Other shops might sell all kinds of things. There is a big shop in London called Harrods. It sells nearly everything, from a packet of pins to a television set.

Some shops have only one person serving behind the counter. In other shops there may be fifty or a hundred. Look at the picture of the shop below. Then write some sentences that best describe this shop. Make a list of things the shop might sell.

This shop is on a street corner. We sometimes call shops like these corner shops. Think of the shops you know. How many are on street corners? What kind of shops are they?

A sorting game

Before you play this game you need to collect lots of empty packets and labels of things you buy in shops. You also need four or five bigger boxes. Put names on them like the ones in the picture.

The idea of the game is to sort the empty packets and labels and put them in their correct box. When you have finished sorting your packets and labels you then make lists of the things that are in each box.

You can also think of different kinds of labels to put on the boxes. For example, one label might be **cleaning**.

An empty bottle of washing-up liquid or an empty polish tin or a soap powder packet would all go in this box. You could add them to your list under the heading **cleaning**.

Kinds of shops

The pictures below show three different shops. What do they sell? What kind of shops are they?

Draw some shop fronts of your own. Don't put their names on. See if your neighbour can tell you what kind they are. Then write down the names of any shops you know that are like them. Say where they are. For example, you could name the street they are in.

This is a special kind of shop. What is it? Write down the names of some you know.

Looking at shops

Class 2 have been out of school with their teacher. They have been looking at the local shops. What time did they start? How long were they out of school?

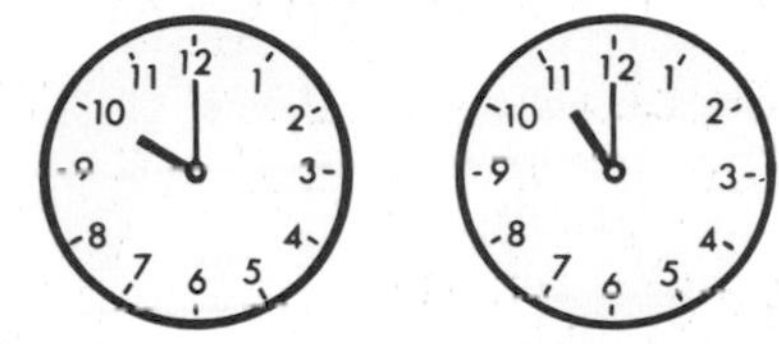

They each had a number of jobs to do when they were out. One was to count the number of shops in a street near the school.

Their teacher gave each boy and girl a plan of the street. They had to mark some of the shops on it. When they got back to school they marked each kind of shop in a different colour on the plan.

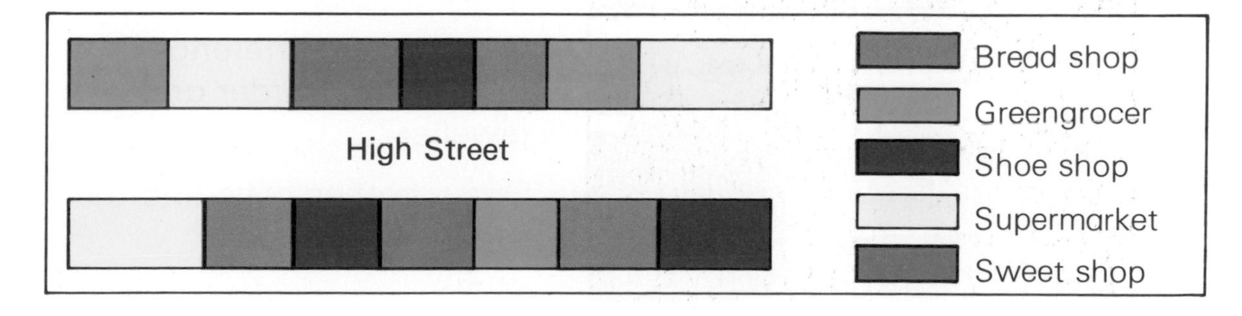

This picture shows shops in a cluster. Write a sentence to say what that means. How many shops are there in this cluster? Some of the buildings are not shops. Write down what they are.

This is a busy area. There are many people and a lot of traffic. Write some sentences to describe what is going on. Do you know a cluster of shops like this? Make a list of the kinds of shops in your cluster. Are they like the shops in the picture?

What is the difference between a warder and a jeweller?

One watches cells and the other sells watches.

Make a big drawing of this plan. It is a plan of the shops in the picture. Colour it in like class 2 did for their shops. Can you show where cars can park on your plan?

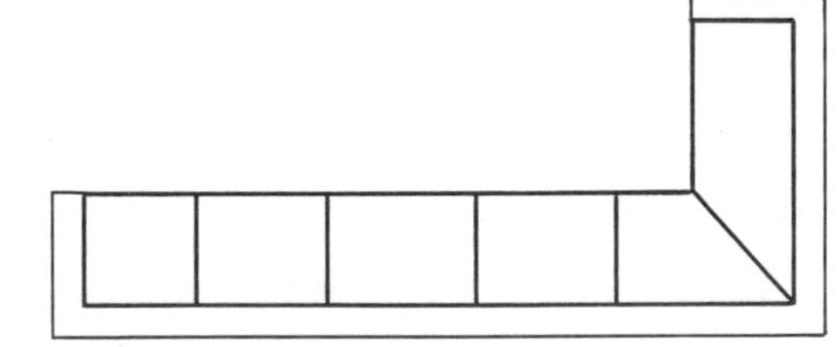
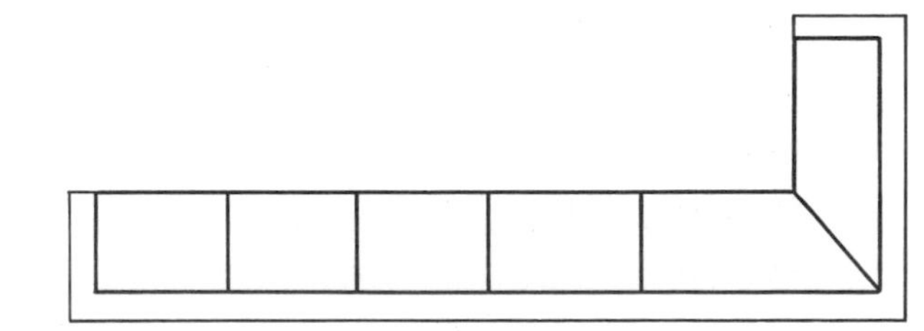

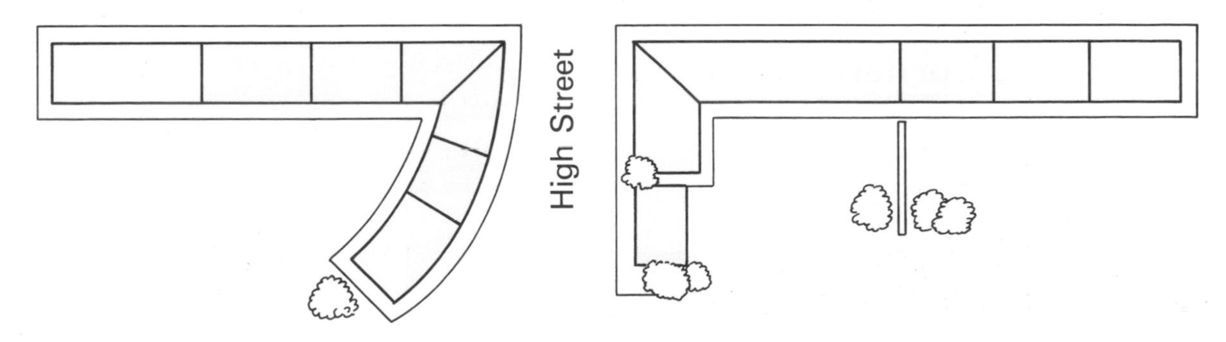

How shops work

Mrs. Green is shopping. She is in the sweet shop on Top Walk. In this shop there are people who serve the customers. They are called shop assistants. Not all shops have assistants. Which shop in Top Walk would not?

Imagine you are going shopping in Top Walk. Make a list of things you want to buy. Next to each one write the name of the shop where you would get it. Put a tick next to the shop where you would serve yourself.

You could make a collection of pictures from magazines to show how shops work.

Use your collection of pictures to help you write a little story. Call it **How shops work.** Here are some words that could be useful:

cash desk	late closing
counter	price tag
customer	queue
deep freeze	sales
delivery van	shop assistant
early closing	supermarket

Puzzle corner

Write down what kinds of shops you can see below.

Copy out these five **heads**. Then complete the sentences by giving each its correct **tail**.

	Head	Tail
1	In big stores there are escalators. These are	a department store called Gums.
2	Cars and lorries are not allowed in some shopping streets. They are called	orders them from a mail order catalogue.
3	Mrs. Green does not go shopping very often because she	pedestrian precincts.
4	The biggest shop in the world is in Russia. It is	moving staircases.
5	When Wendy's mother wants clothes for the children she	has a deep freeze for storing food.

This shop has spilled out on to the pavement. Can you think why?

This packet of cornflakes was the start of a detective story.

Brian's teacher asked him to find out all he could about the packet of cornflakes.

First Brian looked at the packet. It told him who had made the cornflakes and where they were made.

Brian got a map and found the name of the place where the cornflakes were made. The place was called Manchester. It was a city in the north of England.

When he went shopping with his mother, Brian met the manager of the shop that sold the cornflakes.

He told Brian that packets of cornflakes were brought by lorry. Brian saw some of the lorries outside the shop. One of the drivers told him they had come along the motorway from Manchester.

Brian wrote a letter to the factory in Manchester. He told them about his project. They sent him a free booklet. In it was a picture of the factory where the cornflakes were made. He learned that all the maize for the cornflakes was specially grown on farms for the factory.

The booklet also showed him how the packets of cornflakes were filled by machines and then packed in cardboard cases. The cases were stored in warehouses ready for delivery by train or van. The delivery van called every week at the shop. After each delivery the manager filled the empty shelves with fresh packets of cornflakes.

Checking

Thinking

Make a list of the labels and find the missing ones. The pictures below show boxes for the labels. Into which box would you put each label? Are any labels left over? What name would you put on a box for each one left over?

Write down the names of the four boxes. Next to each one put the name of the labels that go in it. How many labels fit the boxes?

Forgetful Freddy

Forgetful Freddy was sent shopping. When he got to the shop he had mixed up the things he needed. He asked for

six sardines
a jar of milk
a litre of jam
a bottle of matches
a tin of yoghurt
a carton of biscuits
a packet of oranges
a box of lemon squash

Write out the list as it should have been.

Doing

John was sent shopping. He started at Woolworths in the High Street, where he bought some soap. He then had to get a cabbage, some nails and a book.

He was told to be careful as the High Street was busy. He must always use the crossings.

Can you follow his journey on page 21? Write down the number of times he used the crossings. Make a list of the shops he went to and the names of the streets they were in.

Design a sign

This is a picture of a shop sign. It tells us what kind of shop we are outside. Draw an interesting picture for a shop sign. See if your neighbour knows what it is.

Going further

Here are some shopping words. They have been mixed up. Can you sort them out?

osikk	k - - - k
equutibo	bo - - - - - e
uspreamkrte	s - - - - - a - - - t
onctioefcnre	co - - e - - i - - er

Look back through the unit. Find some other shopping words. Make them into a **Mixed-up words quiz.**

Detective work

Nearly every packet, box, tin or carton that you buy in shops could be the start of a detective story. Why not try one. Look at page 23 and check how Brian found his clues.

From the label
From a map
At the shop
By writing a letter

Puzzle corner

Where is it? **Clue** – look at the writing.

Copy out and complete the sentences. This picture shows shops in H - - - K - - -. The shop signs are in C - - - - - -. This shows that we find shops all over the w - - - -.

Weather

Clues

First some questions.

What is with us every day and night but we sometimes forget about?

What do a lot of people talk about very often?

What is the one thing that can really spoil a day at the seaside or in the country?

Answer: the weather.

The seven pictures show very different things about the weather. They give us clues to what the weather is like. They might also tell us what has been happening to the weather.

It is easy to tell what has been happening in the first picture. The sky is blue even though it is winter. The snow is deep. It is so deep that cars have become stuck in the snow drifts. The drifts were piled up by strong winds. The snow blower is trying to clear a way through.

Choose the three pictures you find most interesting. Write sentences to say what they show about the weather.

One of the pictures shows another country. There are very bad floods. The country is India. Write a sentence to say what kind of weather makes rivers flood.

If you wanted to have a day out in hot, dry summer weather, which picture would you choose? What are the clues in the picture that show the weather has been hot and dry?

Which picture does the poem describe? Try writing your own weather poem.

Puzzle corner

The weather can be dangerous. Heavy rain can bring floods. People and animals might drown. The weather can be dangerous for aircraft. Do you think the passengers are in danger?

Make a list of ways in which the weather can be dangerous.

Observing

Roger is on his way to school.
He has been caught in the rain.

The clock shows at what time he left his house. Could he have read the weather signs? Look at the picture of Roger leaving his house. Write down what you think the weather signs should have told him.

Roger was not the only one who got caught in the rain. How many other children were not prepared?

Roger's teacher was not happy that so many children had got wet. They had to take their coats off to get them dry. She thought some children would catch a cold if they kept their wet clothes on in school.

'We must learn to read the weather signs,' she said.

'But we don't know them, Miss,' said Roger and the others.

'All right. Let's do a project to learn about them.'

As it was raining, they began that afternoon to find out about rain.

First they watched the rain and talked about it. They noticed how big the drops were and whether the rain came straight down or at a slant. They put a tin can outside to catch the rain. When it had stopped raining they measured how much water was in the can.

They looked outside and made a list of all the things that kept the rain off them: the roof, an umbrella, the porch.

Can you think of any more? Make your own list.

'What happens to the rain after it falls?' asked Julie. The children kept a careful watch and wrote down their answers. They saw how the rain ran off the roof outside and watched where it went.

Here is a clue to where the water went from the roof.

What names would you give to **1** and **2** in the picture?

The children found out what they were made of. Those on the school roof were new and were different from the old ones on the houses nearby. The old ones were made of iron and were very heavy. The new ones on the school were much lighter. They did not need painting.

As the water came down the spouts, class 2 were able to see it run into the grates. Here it was joined by water trickling from the puddles in the playground.

The teacher showed them a picture she had taken two kilometres from the school. It showed where the water from the school flowed into a ditch.

Can you write some sentences about the journey of a raindrop?

Next time it rains, do the things that Roger's class did:

watch the rain
describe it
collect it in a can
measure it
trace its journey

Recording

The pupils in Roger's class finished their project on rain by going to see Roger's uncle. His job was to keep an eye on the weather. He was a meteorologist.

Every day he had to write down in a book what the weather was like. He had instruments to help him.

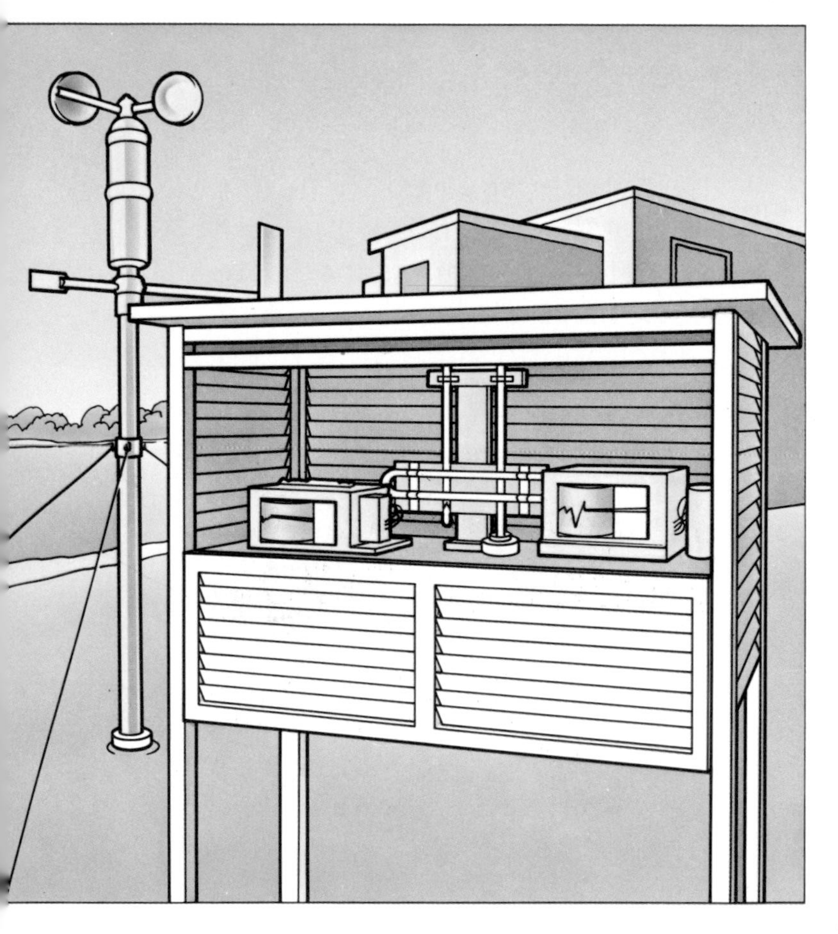

This was where some of the instruments were kept. One was a thermometer. It was used for telling how hot or cold it was. Roger's class did not stay looking at it for long. They were more interested to see how the meteorologist measured the rain.

Nearby, the children saw another instrument. Roger recognized it. It was like the tin can his class used in their project. Can you remember what it was used for? If you can't, look back at page 29.

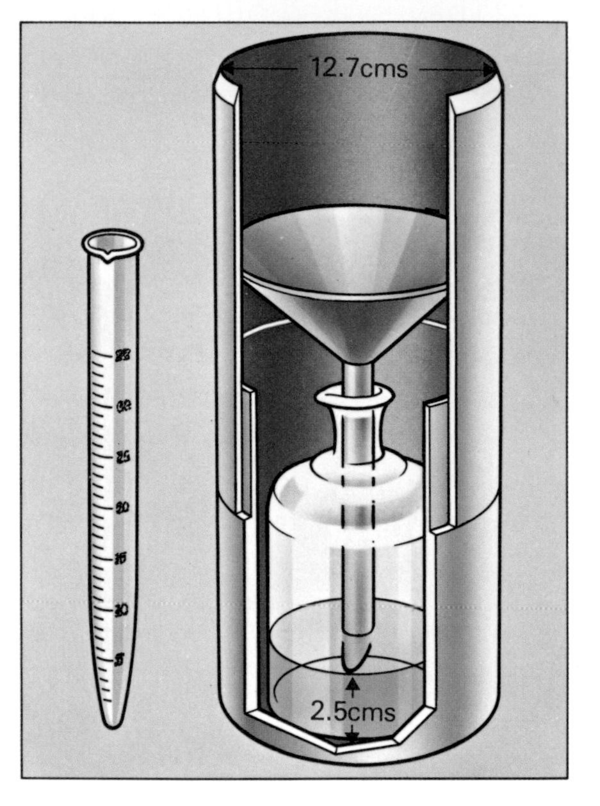

Inside the can was a funnel. It was made of copper so it would not rust. If it had been made of iron or steel, the water would have made it rusty.

You can check this by getting a saucer of water, a new penny and a nail. Put the penny and the nail in the water. The penny is made mainly of copper. The nail is made of iron. Check them after a week, and again after a fortnight. Write some sentences to say what has happened.

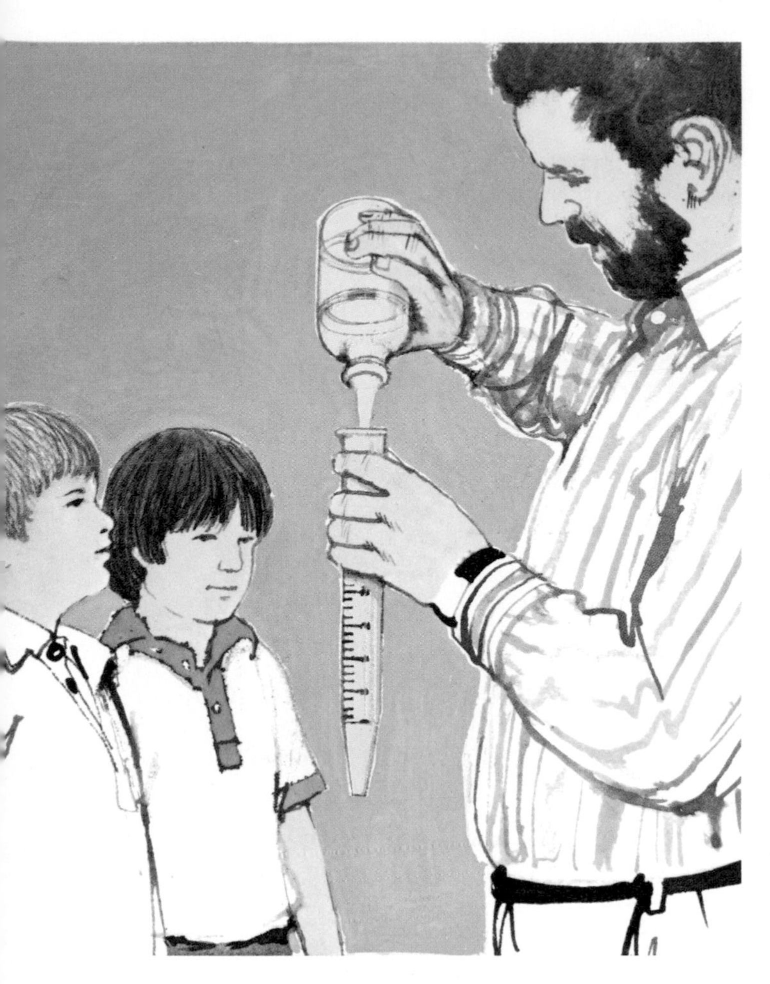

Roger's uncle let the children see how he measured the rain every day. He took the can from the ground and poured the water from it into a bottle. The bottle had marks on the side. Each mark was one millimetre apart.

After he had emptied the can he looked to see how many millimetres of water were in the bottle. He wrote this in his book.

Find a ruler with millimetres marked on it. How many millimetres make one centimetre?

When they had seen how the rain was measured, the children went inside. There they saw how to put the information on a chart.

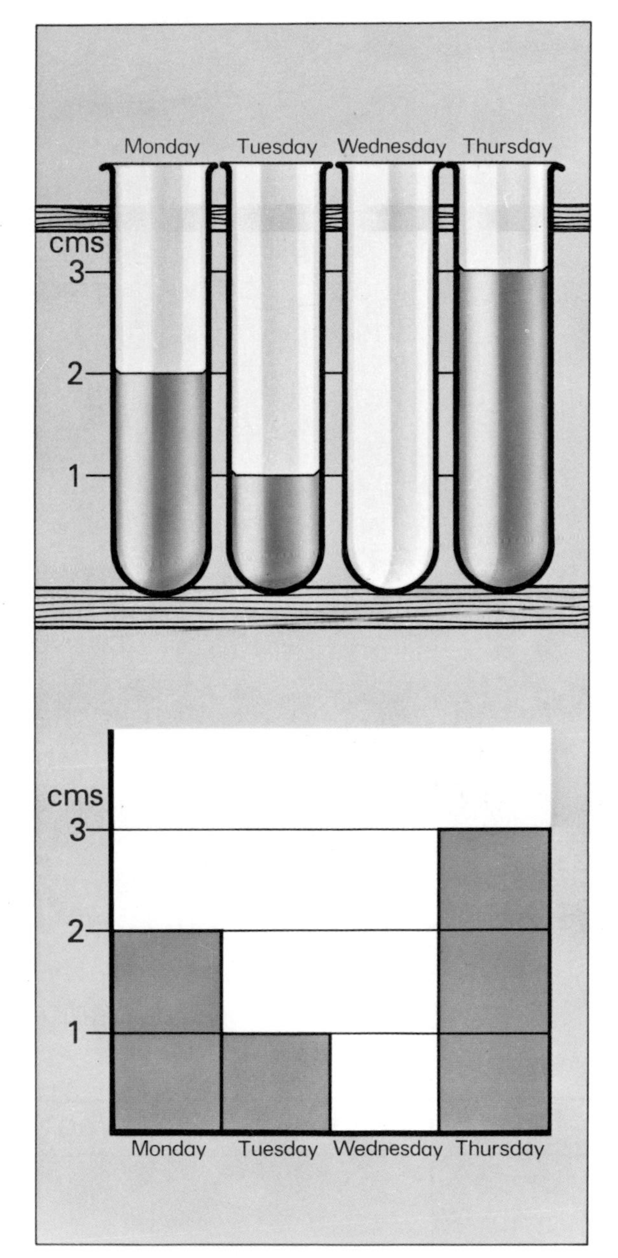

It had been very wet for three of the four days. Which was the wettest day? Which was the driest?

Checking

Thinking

Farmers, fishermen, sailors and many others are interested in the weather. Rhymes have been made about it. This is one.

Red sky at night,
Shepherd's delight.
Red sky in the morning,
Shepherd's warning.

This means we think it is going to be a fine day tomorrow if the sky is red when the sun sets. Copy out the rhyme. Write a sentence to say what it will be like if the sky is red early in the morning.

You can check whether these sayings are true. Look at the sky in the late evening and early morning for a week. Make a note of the colour. Draw a chart like this and write on it the colour of the sky and what the weather was like.

Day	Colour of Sky	Weather
Monday morning		
Monday evening		

It is 9 o'clock in the evening. What will the weather be like tomorrow?

Doing

Get a strip of paper 140 centimetres (56 inches) long. Fasten it on the wall in your classroom. This is how much rain fell in one month on Mount Snowdon in Wales. It is one of the wettest places in Britain. Find it in an atlas. Cut a strip of paper 8 centimetres (3 inches) long. This is how much rain falls in an average month in London.

Draw a picture of three houses, one on top of the other. Enough snow fell in one year in a part of Canada to bury all three houses. How deep was it? Have you ever seen snow that deep? Show how deep the snow was in the worst winter you can remember.

Find Canada in an atlas. The place where the snow was very deep was in British Columbia. What mountains are to be found there? The picture shows them covered in snow. Try to find pictures of other mountains with snow on them. Make a list of their names.

Going further

We all like to go on holiday. Every year a lot of people go to Spain. It is hot in Spain. You could go swimming every day if you wanted to.

Does your class like the sun? Ask each person in the class this question:

'What kind of weather do you like best of these three: hot and sunny; cold and snowy; wet and windy?'

Write the people's names on a sheet of paper. Then make a chart to show the results. Write some sentences to say why you think one kind of weather is the most popular.

Do you like snow?

The people in the picture are skiing. A lot of people go skiing. They go to countries like Scotland and Switzerland.

They usually go in the winter. That is why skiing is called a winter sport. Make a list of other winter sports.

One of Roger's friends sent a weather picture to BBC television. Each day there is a weather report on television. It is shown with the news. Watch it for a few days.

Then choose any kind of weather and draw some pictures the weatherman might use to show viewers what the weather is like.

If it was very windy you could show a yacht with big sails being blown through the waves. Or you could show trees with broken branches.

You might show a boy flying his kite if you wanted to show a breeze.

This is a weather picture. Can you say what weather it shows?

An English steelworker

1 This is Mr. Bell. He works in a steelworks. He is just arriving.

2 The first thing he must do is to clo
on. To do this he gets a card from the office. It has his name on. He puts it in a machine. This stamps the time on to his card.

3 Mr. Bell has an important job. He is in charge of a furnace. You can see all the controls in his room. He must watch each one very carefully.

4 It is very hot in his room and he gets very thirsty. Can you see why? He often has a drink of tea to quench his thirst.

5 Mr. Bell and his team are in charge of the blast furnace. It is like a giant bath. Instead of water it is full of white hot iron. It is like a bubbling cauldron.

6 The furnace is nearly ready to be emptied. Write some sentences to describe what is happening in this picture.

7 It is a dangerous job. The men must protect themselves. Make a list of the special clothes they wear.

8 There are three of these boxes in Mr. Bell's cabin. Do you know what they are called?

9 This is an important moment. The liquid iron is flowing out of the blast furnace. It is like a white hot river. This process is called tapping the furnace.

10 What time is it? How long has Mr. Bell been at work? What is happening to the molten iron? The big bucket is called a ladle.

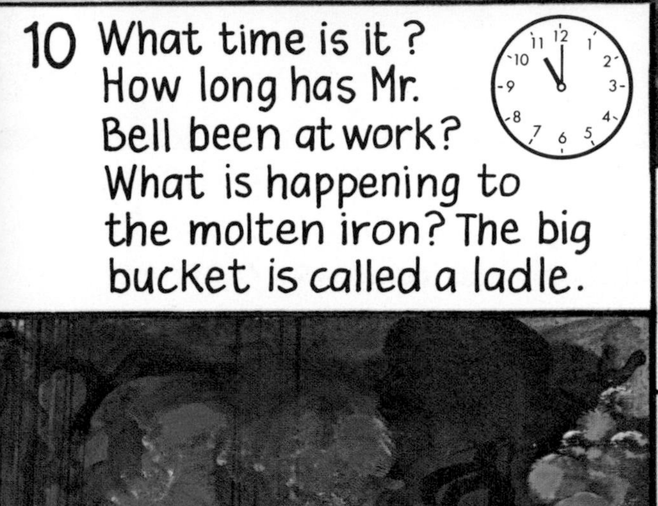

11 This is the crane driver. He is sitting in his control box. The levers control his crane. It is a mobile crane. It runs along tracks.

12 The crane driver's job is to lift the ladle. He must be very careful.

Imagine you are the crane driver. What would you be thinking about? These ideas might help you.

Which lever have I got to use to raise the ladle? Are the hooks firmly on the ladle? I must wait until Dave gets out of the way before I lift the ladle. I must make sure there are no trucks near the crane. Is the ladle level? If not, some of the hot liquid might spill on one of the men below.

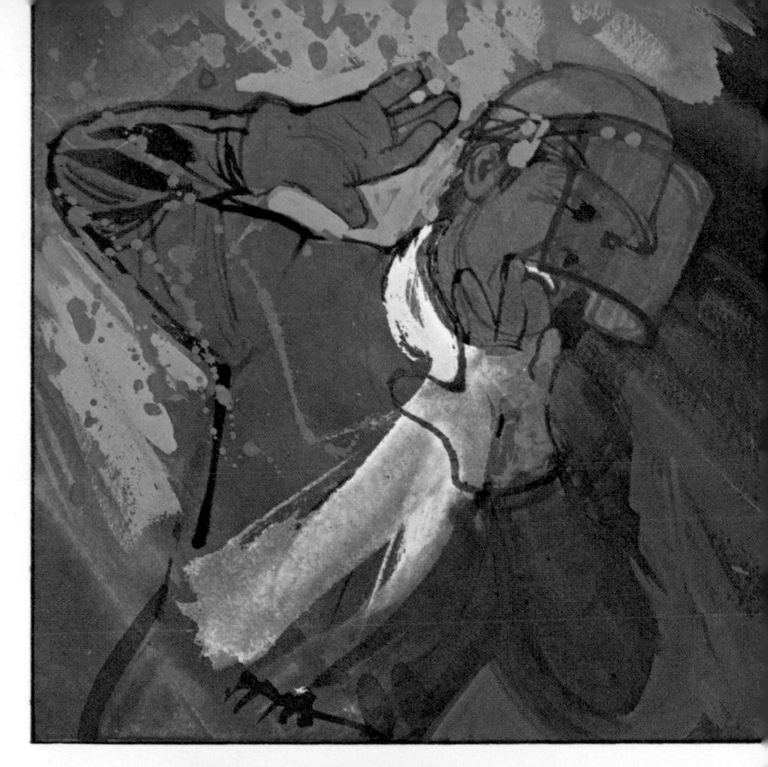

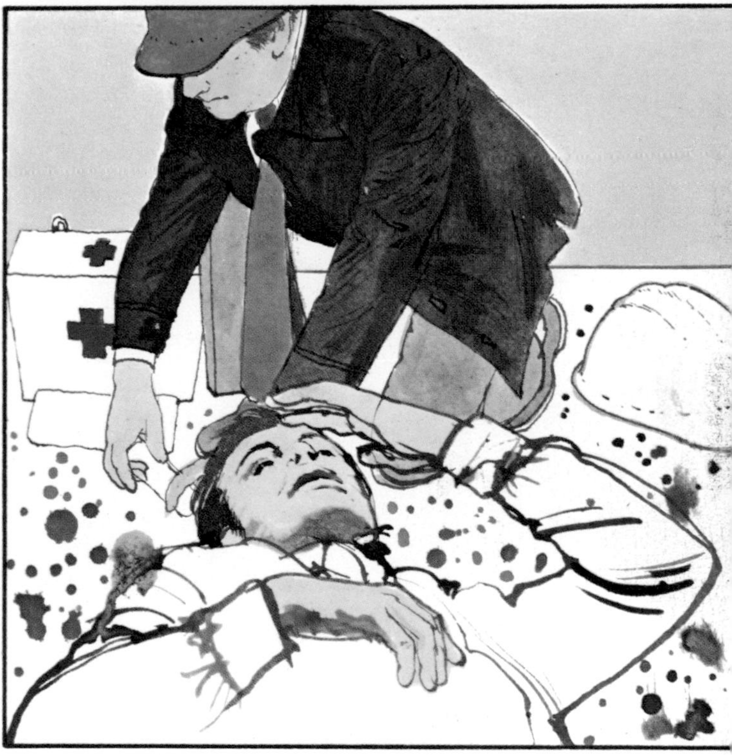

These signs are all over the steelworks. There must be a hundred ways a person could get hurt in a steelworks. Can you think of some? Look back at the pictures to help you. Make a list of them.

Opposite is a picture of an accident. One of the men has been burnt. A piece of hot metal has hit him on his face. As the furnace was being tapped, some of the hot metal spurted up. The man lifted his hands to protect himself.

Mr. Bell got out the first aid box. The doctor came from the works hospital. The man was taken to the hospital for treatment. He was not badly burnt. What do you think saved him?

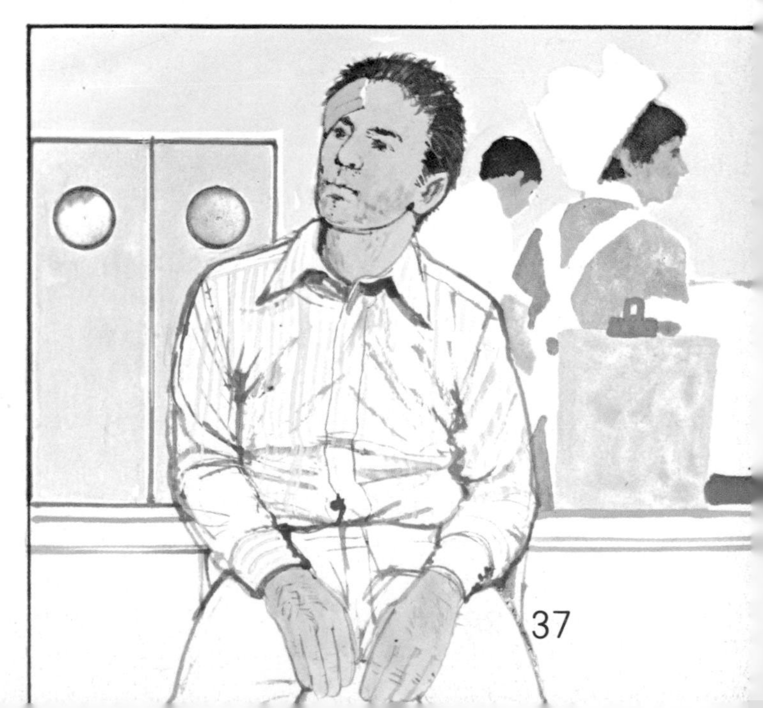

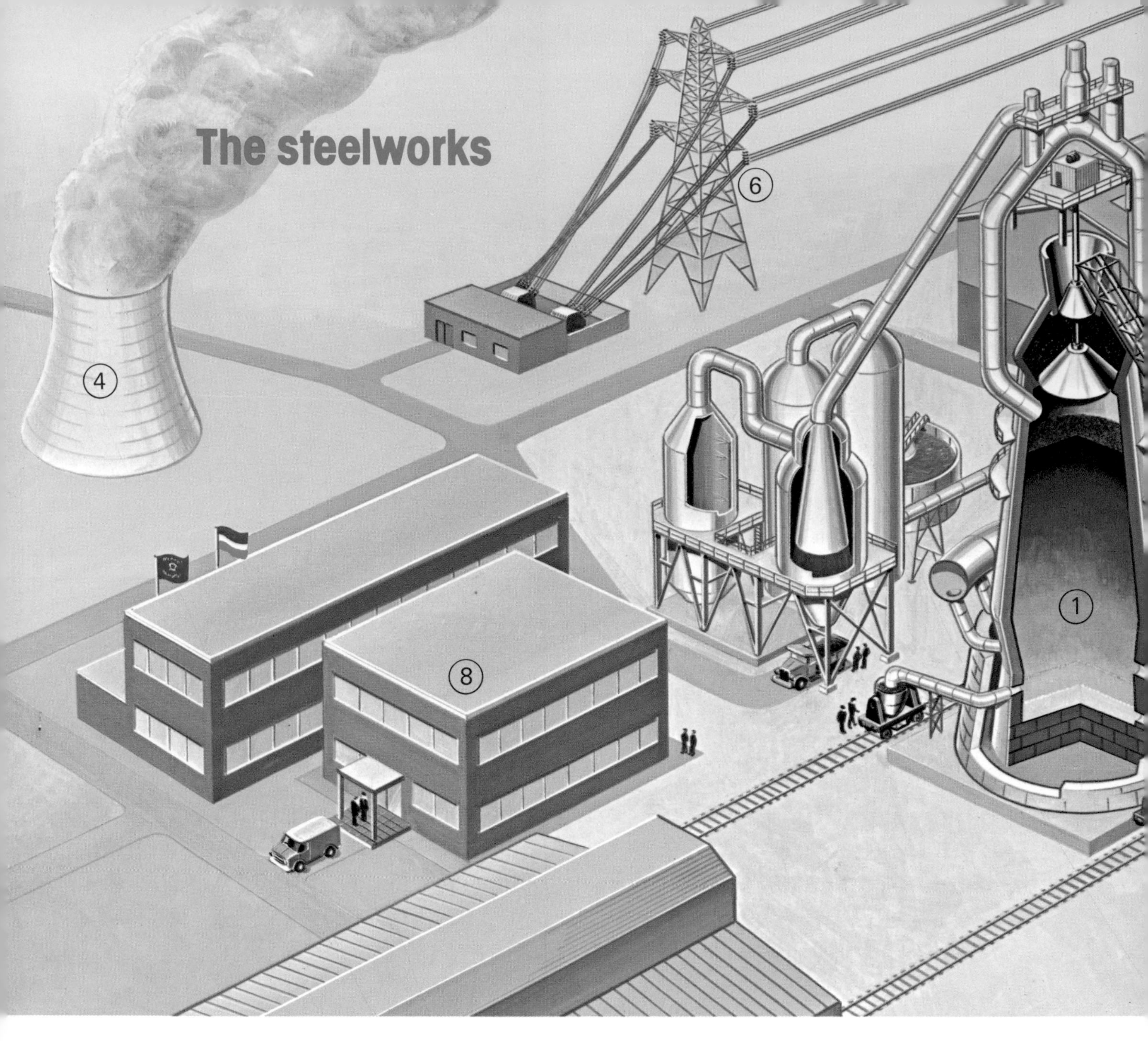

1. This is the blast furnace. Mr. Bell and three other men take turns to be in charge. They work in shifts. Mr. Bell is on the day shift. He works from six o'clock to two o'clock. How long is this?

2. Nearby there are huge piles. They are higher than a house. They are like piles of thick, brown dust. It is iron ore. It was a rock that has been crushed by great machines.

3. The iron ore is brought to the works in trains. It is carried in special waggons. They can be tipped to empty out the iron ore.

4. What is this that looks like a giant egg cup? It is called a cooling tower. Water that is being used in the steelworks gets very hot. It is cooled inside this tower. What are the white clouds above the cooling tower in the picture?

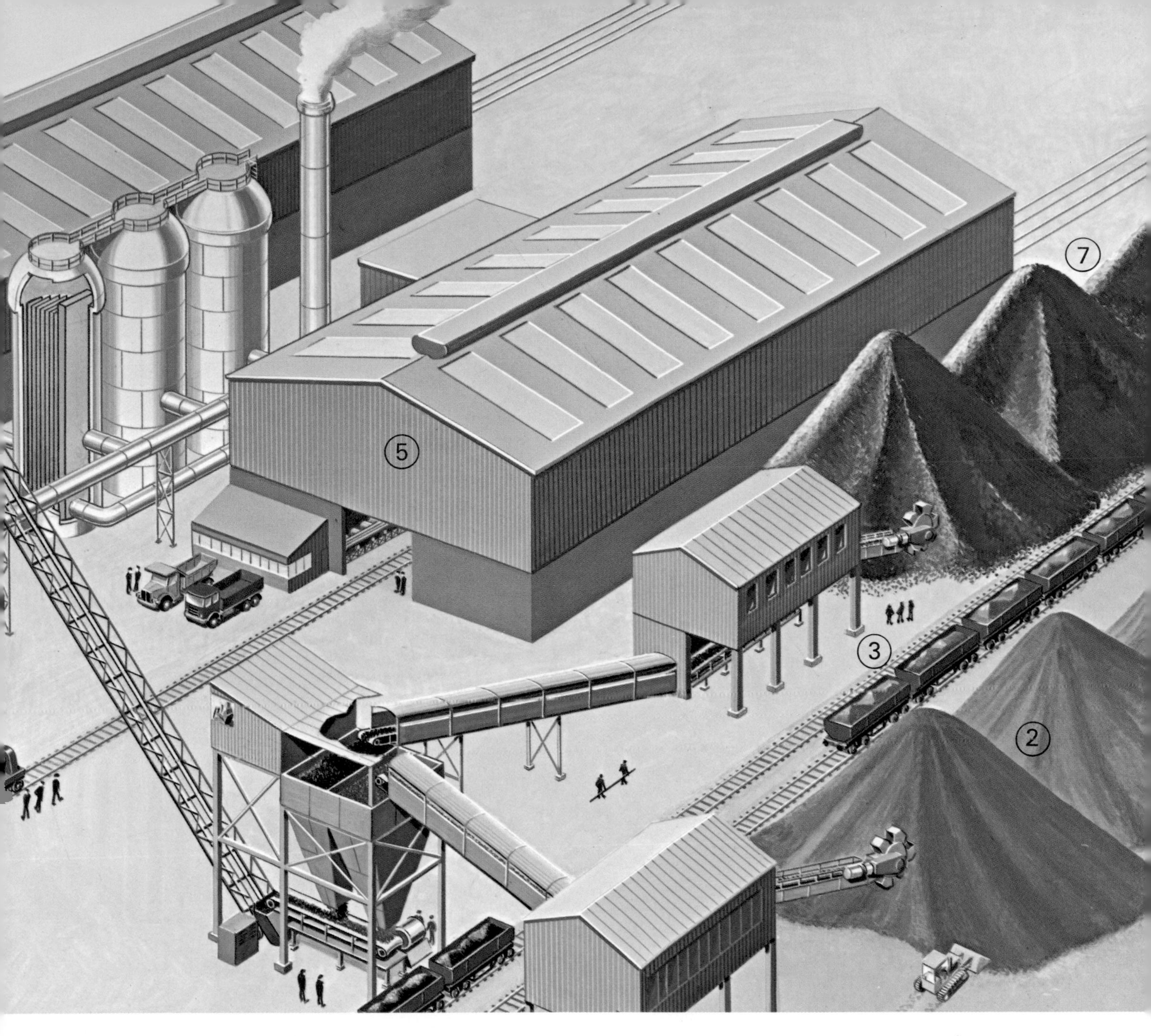

5 Once the metal comes out of the furnace, the men let it cool. It becomes hard and is put between huge rollers which press it into thin sheets. This is done in these sheds.

6 Do you recognize this? What is it called? Why do you think they need electricity in the steelworks? Under the heading **Uses of electricity in the steelworks** make a list of ways in which electricity is used.

7 This huge pile of coke is as big as the piles of iron ore. Look back to pages 34 and 35. What would the coke be used for?

8 At the end of each week Mr. Bell collects his wages from the works office.

Checking

Thinking

Class 2 are looking round their classroom for things made of iron and steel. They are making a list of them. Roger has found one – the dustbin.

Look round your classroom for things made of iron and steel. Make a list of them.

Look back over the unit. Write some sentences about Mr. Bell's job at the steelworks.

Mr. Bell's wife works at the steelworks. She is a typist in the pay office. Make a list of other jobs women might do in a steelworks.

Doing

This is a plastic carton. Make two small holes in the side near the top. Fix a small piece of wood or metal in the holes. This could be a ladle.

Check what it is used for in a steelworks. Use string and two hooks. Put the hooks on the ladle. Put the string over the edge of a chair. Now you can lift the ladle like they do in the steelworks. Is it easy?

Talking

Imagine you are the Safety Officer in the steelworks, and your friend is Mr. Bell.

Tell him how he can help to prevent accidents. For example, you could tell him he must always wear his goggles to protect his eyes. Use the pictures to find some more ideas.

Going further

There are a lot of things made of iron and steel in the home. Make a list of the ones in the pictures on the right. Can you think of any more?

Collect pictures of things made from iron and steel. Stick them on a big sheet of paper. Make them into a classroom display called **Things made of steel.**

The picture below shows one way of making music. What is it? In what part of the world is it popular?

Spotting shapes

You could spot these shapes in a steelworks. What are they? Check them with the picture on pages 38 and 39.

Answer: railway line, waggons, blast furnace, cooling tower, pile of iron ore.

A Brazilian steelworker

This man works in a steelworks. It is a long way from England. It is in a country called Brazil. It is in South America.

His name is Senhor Lima. Senhor is the Portuguese word for Mister. We can call him Mr. Lima or use his first name, Pedro.

You can guess what Pedro would be in English. These pictures show the steelworks where he works.

Look carefully at the pictures on this page. Look back at the English steelworks. Pick out the things that are the same. Make a list of them.

At work

Pedro goes to work five days every week. He starts at six o'clock in the morning. He finishes at two o'clock in the afternoon.

It is very hot in the steelworks. Pedro looks very hot. He often uses a large rag to wipe his face and forehead. It can be very uncomfortable for him if it gets too hot. That is why he likes to have a shower when he has finished work. It makes him feel fresh.

He is in charge of the blast furnace. His job is like Mr Bell's. Can you say what it would be like in his cabin? If you looked around this steelworks you would see signs. They would say:

What do you think they mean? Look back at page 37 if you are not sure.

Pedro is having a meal of meat and beans at work. A lot of people in Brazil eat beans instead of potatoes.

This is Pedro at home. He is having a rest after work. Is his house the same as yours? Are there any things you can see that are different?

1 It is Sunday. This is the only day in the week when Pedro joins his family for breakfast.

2 On Monday Pedro leaves home at half past five in the morning. He goes to work in his car. What kind of car is it? He goes to work with his friend Dicto.

3 His friend Dicto works in the big shed. He works on the huge rollers. Which picture on page 42 shows you the rollers? Write a sentence to say what they are used for.

Steelworks

Steelworks are very noisy places. All over the works you would hear noises like thud, bang, clash, boom.
The rollers are humming.
The hot steel is hissing.
There is thunder and lightning.
Bright lights are flashing.
The men at the furnace are sweaty and sticky.

Use the pictures to help you write some more sentences like these about a steelworks.

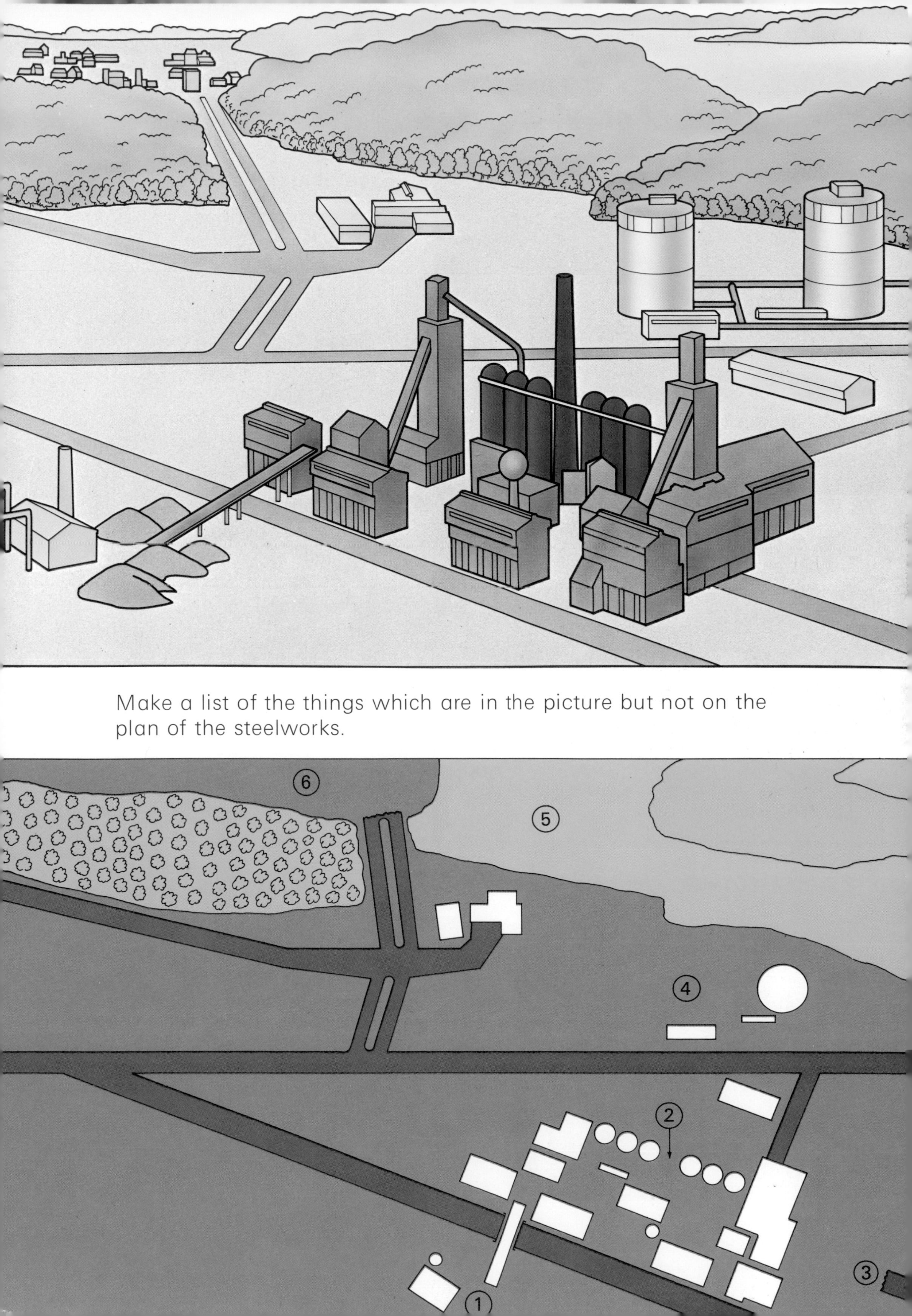
Make a list of the things which are in the picture but not on the plan of the steelworks.
6
5
4
2
3
1

Uses of steel

Steel is used in Brazil . . .

. . . to make **bridges.** This is part of one of the longest bridges in the world. It is also one of the highest. Large ships can still sail under it. It is built mainly of steel. There are thick steel plates inside each support. You can see other uses of steel. For example, steel cranes were used to build the bridge.

. . . to make **dams**. This one has been built to make a lake. The water in the lake is used for drinking. The water is sent along huge, steel pipes to the towns. Most of the dam is made of concrete but this is made stronger with steel rods.

. . . to make **buildings**. Can you see where steel is used to make these buildings? What name do we give to very tall buildings in cities?

Make a list of the things made of steel on this page. Then find out the names of ten more things made of steel. Add them to your list.

You could show how a tall building is made by using straws in place of steel.

To do this you would need about twenty straws, some scissors, paste, plain paper and felt tips.

1 First cut four straws into 10 centimetre lengths. Then cut twenty-four pieces. Make each one 5 centimetres long.

2 Lay two long straws on a piece of paper and fix six short ones to them with glue.

3 Do the same with the two other long and six short pieces of straw. Stand the pieces up and glue on the other twelve pieces.

4 Cut out a piece of paper 10 centimetres by 20 centimetres. Carefully fold it in four.

5 Use felt tips to mark on windows and doors. Then glue it to the straw frame. You now have a building. It is like a skyscraper or tower block. The straws are in place of the thick, steel girders that are used to make tall buildings.

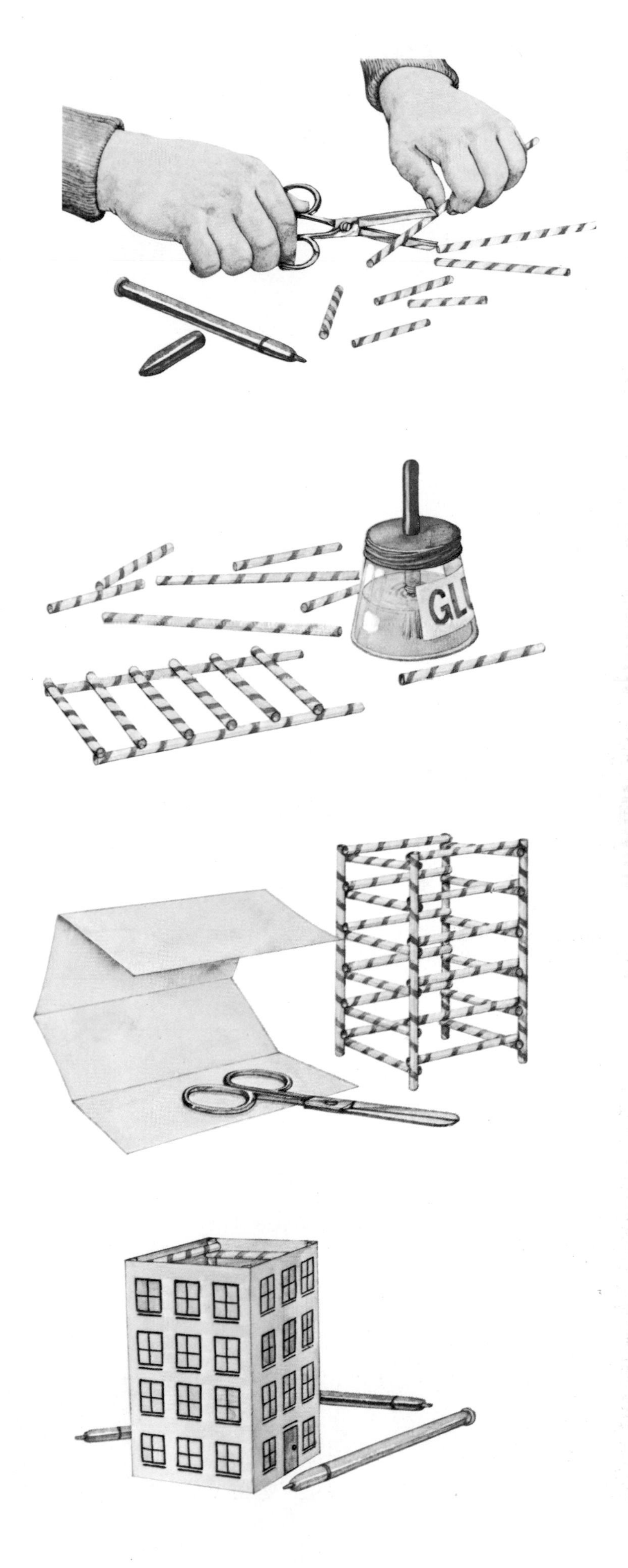

Checking

Thinking

		Mr. Bell	Mr. Lima
1	In which country does he live?	p.48	p.42
2	What is his first name?	John	p.42
3	What language does he speak?	English	p.42
4	How many children has he?	Four	p.49
5	What is his job?	p.34	p.43
6	Is his job dangerous?	p.37	p.43
7	What signs are put up in the works?	p.37	p.43
8	Does his wife work?	p.40	No
9	How does he go to work?	In his car	p.44
10	What is his favourite sport?	Football	p.49

Make a copy of the chart. Find the answers and put them in the spaces. Some have been done for you.

Protective clothes

Copy out the numbers and put labels next to each. Write some sentences to say why steelworkers wear them.

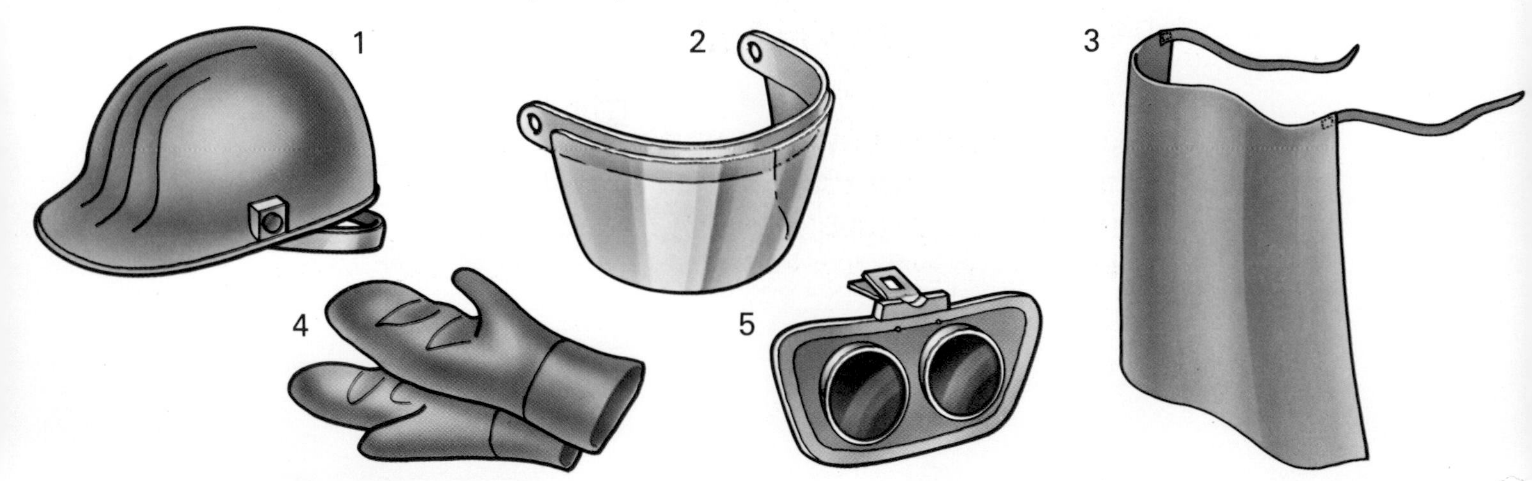

Going further

One of Pedro's favourite games is football. He takes his son Nico to watch the matches.

One of Nico's favourite players is Pele. He used to play for Brazil. He was one of the most famous footballers in the world.

Mrs. Lima and her daughter would rather go to the beach. There are many beautiful beaches in Brazil. It is very hot.

A lot of the best beaches are near the city of Rio de Janeiro. Janeiro is the name of a month. Guess which one. If Rio means river, what do you think the name Rio de Janeiro means?

Pedro and his family go there for holidays. The children like to go when it is carnival time. People dress up. They have big parades on the streets. They dance and sing for a whole week.

Can you make a list of carnival words? The picture will help you. Here are some to start you off: band, happy people, streamers, dancing.

The docks

Every day Bill Hughes goes in this little boat to meet the big ships in Liverpool Bay. He has a very important job. He is a river pilot.

He has just reached the ship. It has come from Canada. Bill takes over from the ship's captain. His job is to steer the ship up the river. He has been specially trained to do this.

This is what he sees as he looks out of the ship's window. He points out some of the famous buildings to the ship's captain. They can see the tall buildings with birds on top. These are the famous Liver birds.

As they sail towards Liverpool, they pass some of the docks. There are some ships in the docks. The pilot knows all the ships by the flag painted on the funnel. Each one is different.

The water is shallow in some parts of the river. That is why the pilot is needed. He knows where every sandbank is. If a ship hit a sandbank it might sink.

These are buoys. They are fixed in the river. Each is a signal to the pilot. He knows there is a wrecked ship under the water. He keeps clear of them.

This is an oil tanker. It has just arrived. The men are fixing pipes on to the tanker. These will be used to unload the oil.

Work in the docks

Ships carry all kinds of things – oil, cars, bananas, wheat, and lots more. Here are pictures of six things that ships carry. What are they?

A load of bananas coming off a ship.

After the pilot has brought the ship into dock, the dockers take over. The men who unload ships are called dockers. They work in teams. At one time most things were unloaded by hand. It was very hard work. The men had to be strong. They had to lift heavy weights.

These pictures show how things have changed. How do these machines help the docker in his work?

You can collect pictures of things brought in ships from other countries. You will find plenty in magazines.

Make a scrapbook for your collection. Write two labels for each picture. One should say what it is. The other should give the name of the country it comes from. It might be butter from New Zealand, bacon from Denmark or oranges from Cyprus.

This is a picture of the docks. We have cut away part of it so that you can see inside the ship and the building. The ship is tied up in the dock. It is being unloaded.

The numbers on the labels have been mixed up. Write them so the number is next to the correct label.

1 Shed
2 Water
3 Cargo
4 Ship
5 Rail truck
6 Crane
7 Mobile crane
8 Floating crane

Containers

A container is a very large box. It is very strong. It is made of wood and steel.

Containers are used for carrying things. Each container is packed at a factory. It may contain a load of clocks, engines, furniture or tyres. When the container is full it is locked for safety.

A ship can carry hundreds of containers at a time. Estimate the size of this container. How many would fit in your classroom?

Cargoes

Things carried in a ship are called its cargo. Look back at pages 52 and 53. Make a list of ships' cargoes from these two pages.

When a ship arrives, its cargo is unloaded in the docks. There are different ways of lifting cargo from the ship.

Containers have square holes in each corner. A special crane is used. It has four hooks. One goes in each hole. Then the crane lifts the container out of the ship straight on to a lorry that is waiting to take it away.

If a cargo is very heavy a floating crane is used. It comes near the ship. The jib is lowered and then the heavy weight is picked up with steel chains. These cranes can lift a railway engine out of a ship.

Some cranes have special hooks for lifting flat, wooden trays. The trays are called pallets. These are piled with boxes. This saves time in unloading. The crane does not lift each box one at a time; it lifts one pallet that has ten boxes on it.

When a ship's cargo is sugar, it can be unloaded by grabs. These are like huge scoops. The crane lowers them into the sugar. The big steel jaws of the scoop are opened and then closed. The crane lifts it out of the ship and pours the sugar from the scoop into a waiting lorry.

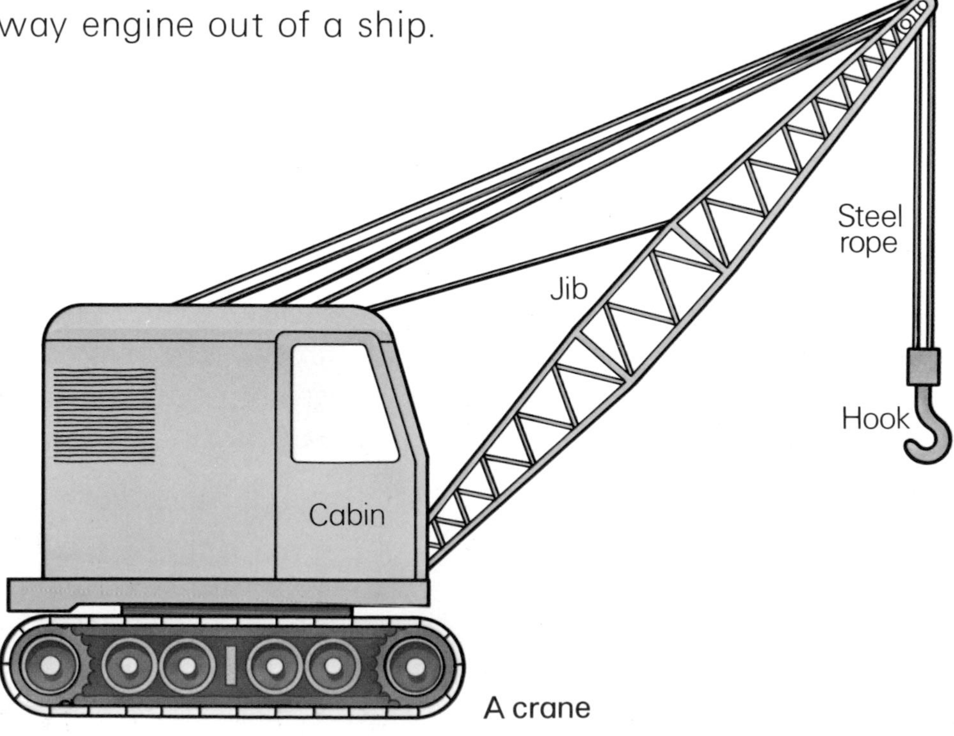

A crane

1 Diesel engine – Pallet
2 Containers – Scoop
3 Sugar – Floating crane
4 Boxes of oranges – Chain and hooks

Sort out the labels and match them to the correct number.

Tankers

A ship which carries oil as a cargo is called a tanker. Tankers bring oil to Britain from other countries.

Tankers are usually big ships. Some of the biggest ships in the world are tankers. Their cargo can be very dangerous. Do you know why?

When Bill Hughes pilots a tanker he is extra careful. He knows that one mistake could be dangerous. There are many things that could go wrong.

On the next page there is a game. It is called **the tanker game.** To play it you need dice and a counter. You will also need a piece of paper and a pencil.

The tanker game
Start
1
2
Fog
3
4
5
Gales
6
11
The Captain falls sick
10
9
Engine trouble
14
Wreck shifts in storm
15
16
17
Dockers on strike
18

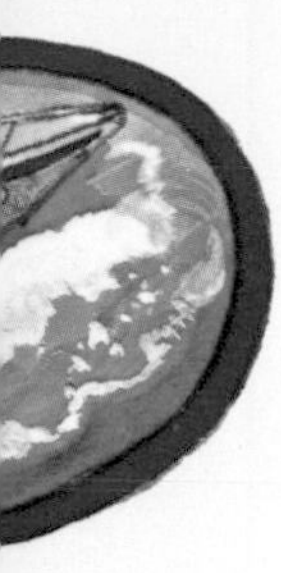

Rules

Make a copy of the pilot's log book.

1 Put a ring round day 1. That is when you start.
2 If you throw a four, move your counter four spaces and so on, until you finish. Put a tick in your log book for each square you land in.
3 If you land on a red number, you miss a turn and put a ring round the next day.
4 At the end see how many days and hours you took. Were you held up? Why?

Pilot's log book				
Days	Hours			
Day 1	1		13	
	2		14	
Day 2	3		15	
	4		16	
Day 3	5		17	
	6		18	
Day 4	7		19	
	8		20	
Day 5	9		21	
	10		22	
Day 6	11		23	
	12		24	

A dustman

Evening

This is Jim Jones. He likes to play bowls in the evening. His wife and daughter are watching him.

Next day

Early next morning Jim arrives at work. Does the picture give you a clue to what his job is? What time does he start?

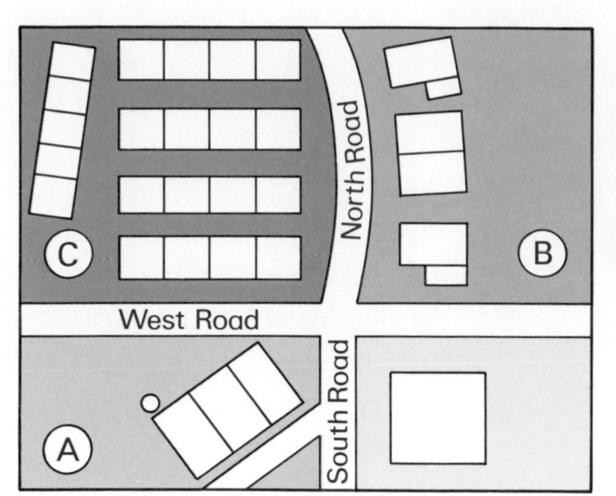

He is a dustman. Dustmen are sometimes called refuse collectors. Before Jim begins work today, he has to look at the plan. He wants to check where he is working. He is going to work in area **B**.

Spotting shapes.

A hawk's eye view of ______
Can you say what it is?
Two clues – Mr. Jones travels in it every day he is at work. His mate Fred is in the picture.

Try drawing a different hawk's eye view of something. See if your friend knows what it is.

Answer: a dustcart. Next to it are two dustbins. They are round. A dustman is shown. He is wearing a cap. You can see the tips of his boots.

Today Jim will drive his dustcart along South Road and into North Road. He will start at the end house. It is number 36. Find it on the picture. What kind of house is it? Copy out and finish these two sentences. Jim Jones is a ______ or ______.
The first house he calls at is ______.

Jim is the driver. He works with Fred and Bert. Their job is to empty the dustbins.

Bert talks to Fred

But they both had to go the long way round. Look at the picture at the top of the page. Write some sentences to say why they had to go the long way round.

Waste and save

Try making up a list of **rubbish words**. Here are some to start you off:

refuse	w - - t -
junk	tr - - h

Why?

Why do we throw things away? The pictures show seven reasons why we throw things away.

These are the answers, but they have been mixed up. Copy them out so that they are in the right order. The first one should be **It is broken.** Now try the rest.

1 Things become too small to wear.
2 We can't eat it.
3 They are used up.
4 It has gone bad.
5 It is worn out.
6 It is out of date.
7 It is broken.

When Jim, Bert and Fred collect rubbish they are careful. If they see . . .

newspapers, they put them in a pile on their own;

tin cans, they use the big magnet back at the depot to lift them out;

bottles, they ask people to put them beside the dustbin so they can collect them in special boxes.

The bottles are crushed and recycled to make new bottles.

The newspapers are shredded in a factory to make ________?

The tin cans are crushed in a factory and used to make ________?

Can you find out the answers? 'Common sense, ain't it?' says Fred. Do you agree?

The car wash

This car is very dirty. It has been a very hot week. Each day Mr. Smith has driven his car in the country. He has visited a lot of farms. The lanes leading to the farms were covered in dust. The car wheels threw it up in thick clouds. A lot of the dust stayed on the car. Mr. Smith takes his car to the garage to have it cleaned. It goes in the car wash. Look at the picture of the car wash. Use the title **The car wash** and put some of these words in sentences to describe it:

drive car up
money in machine
jets of water
huge, fluffy rollers
spin like a
rattling and bumping
misty spray
car shining and clean

When Mr. Smith sees the water running down the drain from the car wash he has an idea . . .

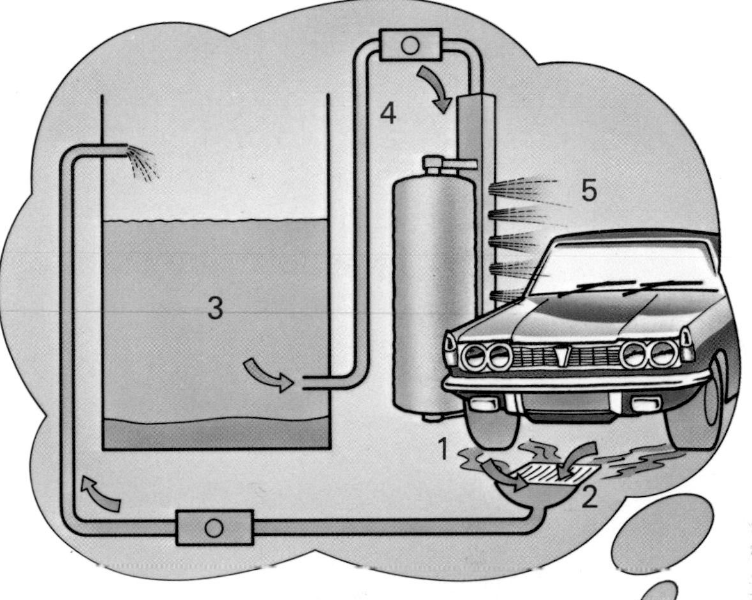

Mr. Smith thinks the water **1** which is going down the drain **2** should not be wasted. Instead it could be pumped into a big tank **3**. It would stay there until the mud settles on the bottom. Then the clean water could be sent along a pipe **4** and used again **5**. Not a drop would be wasted. Do you think it is a good idea?

An experiment

Take a glass of water. Add some soil. Stir it up until the water is muddy. Leave it for a day. Then check the glass. Write some sentences about it. How does this experiment fit into Mr. Smith's idea?

Waste not . . .

What is the other half of this proverb? A proverb is a wise saying. Do you think this one is?

Rubbish and health

Rubbish tip or park

Look at the two pictures at the bottom of the page. In some towns, rubbish tips have been made into playing fields. After the rubbish has been there for a long time it is flattened. Giant bulldozers are used to do this.

A lot of soil is spread over the old rubbish to cover it up. Then grass seeds are planted. When the grass grows, children can play safely on the old rubbish tip.

Imagine you lived in a big city. If all the rubbish was collected for a month, this is what it would look like.

Work out how long, wide and high the heap would be. Imagine what it would be like after a year. It would be twelve times this size!

Rubbish breeds germs. Germs can kill. One reason why we collect rubbish from houses is to help people stay healthy. Germs are so small you cannot see them.

A long time ago a lot of people died in London. At first nobody knew why. Then it was found they all had a disease. It was called cholera. It was caused by germs. Cholera can kill.

But nobody knew what caused the cholera. Then a doctor did some detective work. He found that all the people who died had collected their drinking water from a certain water pump. It was in Broad Street. The people used to go there to fill jugs and buckets because they did not have taps in their houses.

The doctor stopped people using the water pump. This helped to prevent people dying of cholera. Say what you think had been wrong with the water.

Draw a plan of Broad Street, using the two pictures to help you. Mark the pump on your plan.

Checking

Thinking

These six pictures all show waste collected by Jim, Bert and Fred. One day Jim showed his daughter a picture of their district.

'If you can tell me where each of these lots of waste comes from, I will buy you a packet of crisps,' he told her.

'The first would come from **C**. I know that because those houses still have coal fires. There is smoke coming from the chimneys. The other houses must have central heating', said Judy. She was right.

Draw the six pictures. Copy Judy's answer next to the first one. Then work out the other five and write the answers next to the pictures you have drawn.

Going further

Seedling

30 years

Tree

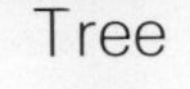

1 year

Factory

1 year

House

10 years

Waste tip

Class 2 made two charts. One showed how a young tree grew into a big tree. It was then cut down. The wood was taken to a factory. There it was made into a chair. The chair was sold in a shop and taken to a house. It got broken and was taken to the waste tip.

They also put **time** on the chart. It took thirty years for the tree to grow. It took one year for the chair to be made. The chair was in the shop for one year before it was bought. It lasted ten years before it got broken.
How long was this altogether?

Make a chart like this. Call it
The story of a woollen blanket
How many years might this story last?

Tell the story of these two objects.

To and from the docks

Mr. Ray has called at the garage. He wants to buy some petrol. 'Four gallons please,' he says to the attendant. The lady opens the filler cap on Mr. Ray's car. She puts the nozzle in and switches on the pump.

How does Mr. Ray know he is getting any petrol?

He has two ways of checking.

He can look at the petrol pump. He can also look at the dial inside his car.

But he does not **see** the petrol going into his car.

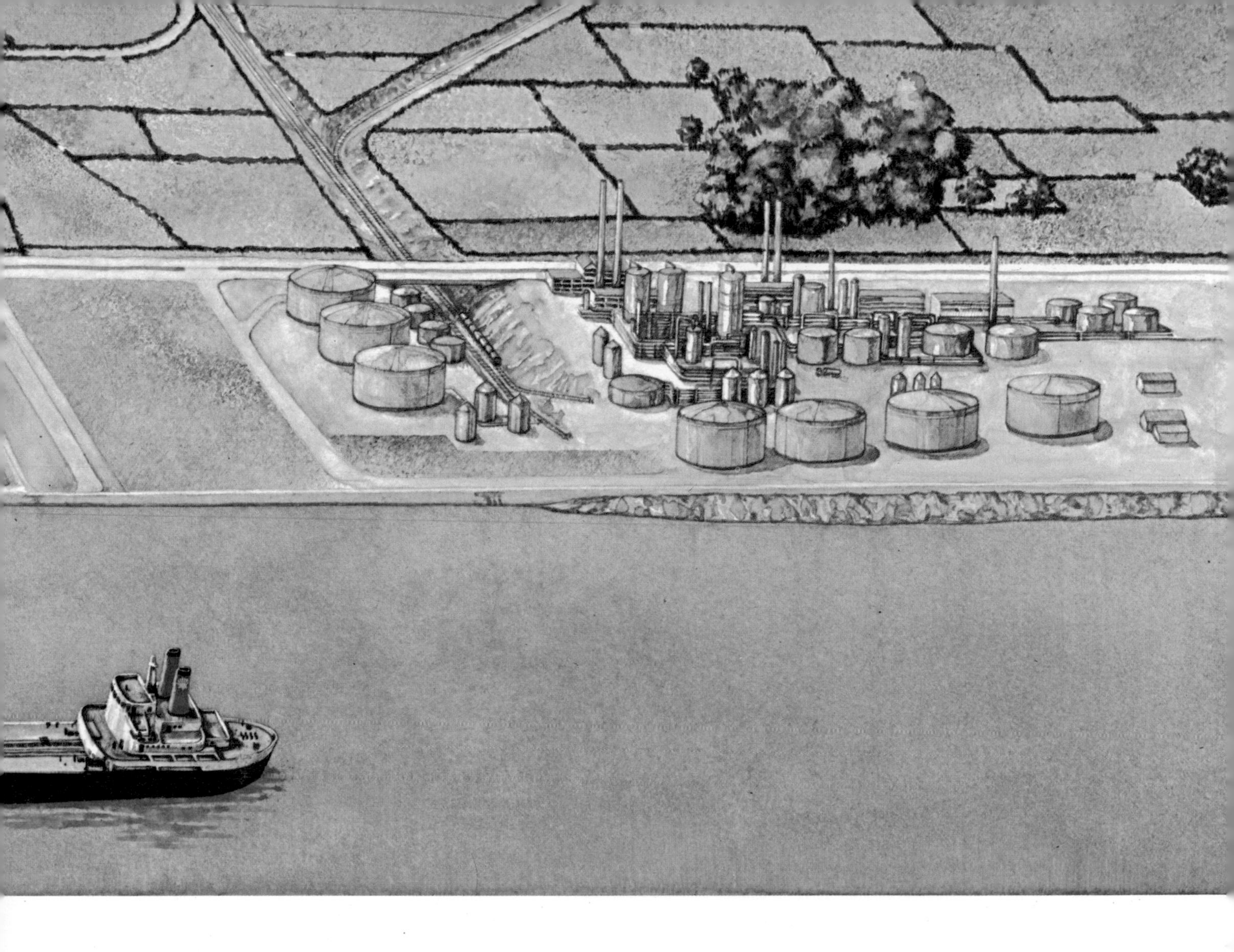

Pipelines

Look at the picture. It shows a tanker in the docks. It is unloading its cargo of oil. Copy out this sentence and complete it. **Oil is called the invisible cargo because** . . .

How would the men know when they had unloaded all the oil?

The pipes lead from the ship to big tanks. What would be in the tanks?

How many shapes can you see in the picture? Try to draw and label some of them.

Puzzle corner

Why are oil pipes not usually visible? The picture gives you a clue. Write some sentences to describe what is happening in this picture.

By road

This ship has come from Russia. Her name is the **M.V. Volga.** It is written on her side. M.V. means motor vessel. She is in the docks at Garston near Liverpool.

Men are busy unloading timber. They use cranes to lift it straight from the ship on to lorries. The lorries pull up on the quay. They stand in a queue. As soon as a lorry is loaded it drives away. The next lorry takes its place.

The dockers will load twenty lorries in a day. The first lorry in the queue is going to Manchester. The next one is taking timber to a sawmill in Chester.

These are nine places where lorries will go to from Garston:

Birmingham
Chester
Coventry
Derby
Manchester
Preston
Sheffield
Warrington
Welshpool

They are all towns. Find them on the map. Which is the nearest to Garston? Which is furthest away? Make a list of the names. Look at the map. Put a tick next to the towns which are more than 40 kilometres from Garston. How many are there?

What is the timber used for? These are four things made of wood. Make a list of them. See if you can think of ten more to add to your list.

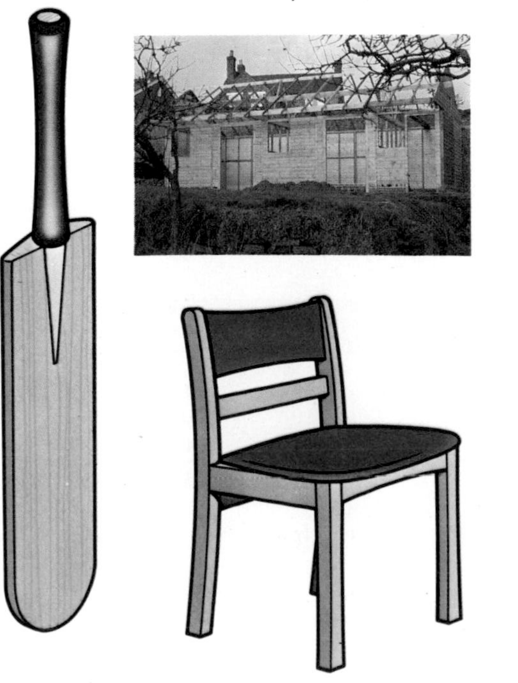

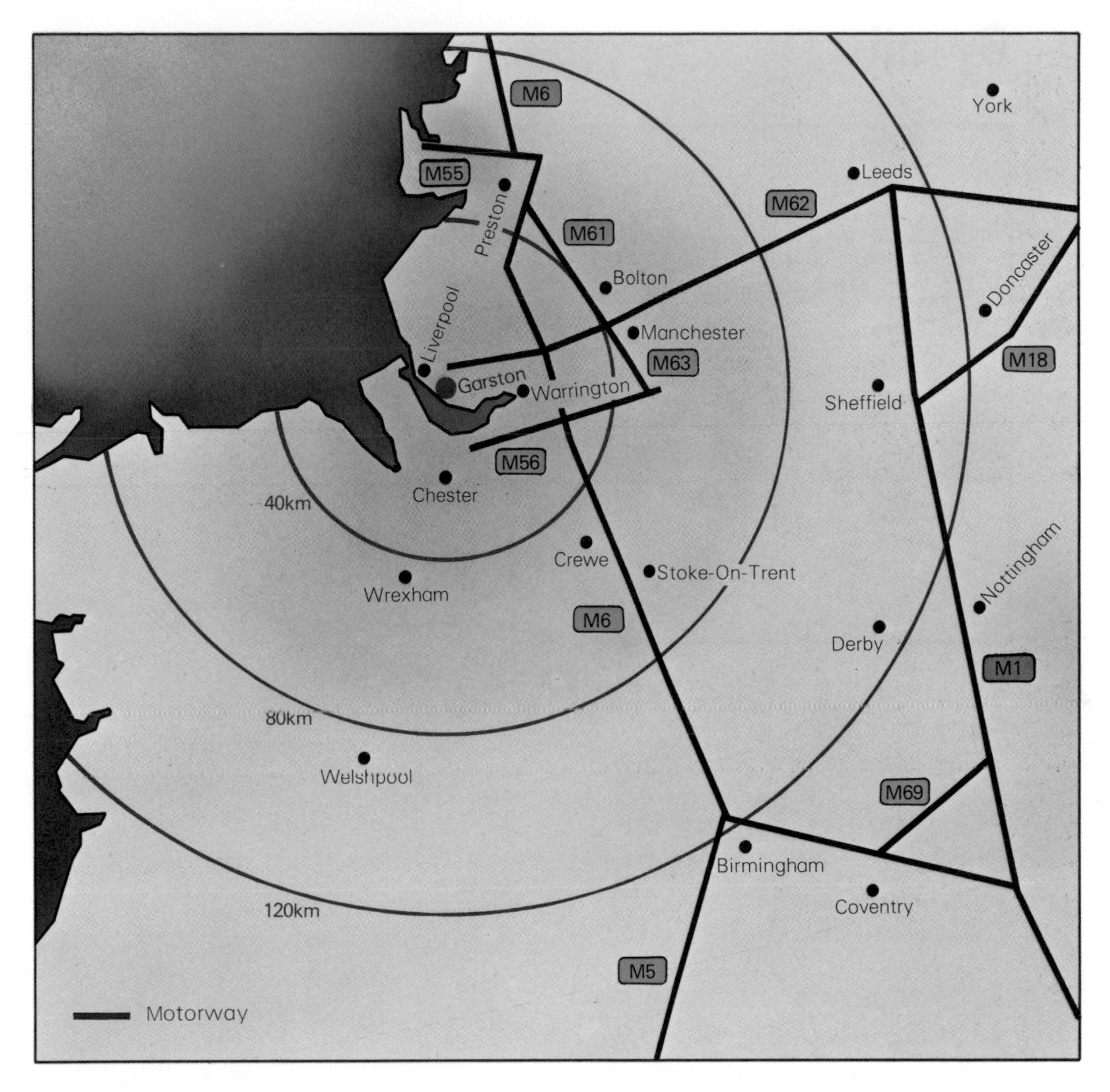

The lorries often go on the motorway. This is the start of a motorway near Liverpool. Would some of the timber lorries use it? **Clue** – look at the map.

Have you been on a motorway? Here is a list of **motorway words.** You can add more of your own.

lorry
road sign
hard shoulder
bridge
fast lane

Write about a journey on a motorway and draw some motorway pictures.

By rail

This is a rail truck. It is loaded with coal. It is part of a trainload of coal.

The train has just left the docks at Vitoria in Brazil. It is going to the steelworks where Pedro works.

Every day four trains loaded with coal leave the docks. The coal is needed in the steelworks to help make the steel.

It is 400 kilometres from the docks to the steelworks. The train travels slowly. It takes nearly a full day to get there. Trains are often used to carry loads that are too heavy for lorries.

This train has special tipper waggons. The coal can be tipped out easily. When the train is empty it is shunted into a siding. Here it is turned round, ready to go back to Vitoria.

It does not go back empty. The waggons are loaded up with iron ore. When the train is full it is driven down to Vitoria. It goes slowly because it is carrying a heavy load. It takes a day to make the journey.

At the docks the iron ore is loaded on to ships by huge cranes. Some of the iron ore goes to steelworks in other parts of Brazil. Some comes to England.

Look at the pictures. What would train **1** be carrying? What would train **2** be carrying? Work out how long a train takes to make the journey from the docks to the steelworks and back again. This is called a round trip. Write a sentence beginning **The round trip takes . . .**

Passengers

Ships carry passengers as well as cargo. Ships which carry people are called liners.

Here is a list of other kinds of ships. The letters have been mixed up. Sort them out and use them to start your own list. Try to find out more about each kind of ship.

knerat	t-n--r
grddree	dr----r
tycha	y--h-
rryfe tboa	f--ry --a-

Some passengers have just left a liner at the docks in Tilbury, near London. They have returned from a cruise. Their home is in Bristol, so they have arrived at Paddington station in London. The train to Bristol leaves from Paddington.

It is a very fast train. It is called the 125. Can you guess why?

Today is a special day. An old steam train is starting off at the same time as the 125. Make a copy of the chart along the bottom of the page and say which is the faster train.

The 125 is an inter-city train. It travels between the cities of London and Bristol. Write a sentence to say what inter-city means. What do you think the British Rail symbol on the side of this train means?

Checking

Thinking

Hidden cargoes

We do not see the oil as it is unloaded. We cannot see it on its journey after it is unloaded. Are there any other hidden cargoes? Make a list of them.

Breakdown

The railway track between Vitoria and the steelworks is a single track. Last week two trains broke down. They were stuck for two days. What would happen to the other trains? The ship in the docks at Vitoria was due to sail at midnight on the Friday. Would it get away on time? Write some sentences to say what you would do to make things better.

Doing

Look at the sign on the ship's funnel on page 67. It is the sign of a famous oil company. You can see it on their garages. Collect the names of other oil companies and pictures of their badges.

Adverts

Next time you see oil adverts on T.V. make a note of them. Write down the name of the oil company. For example, you might see one for Shell or Mobil. These are the names of two oil companies.

Remember that petrol is made from oil. Do the adverts tell you if oil is used for anything else? If they do, keep a note of what it is.

Look in newspapers and magazines. Find adverts for oil and petrol. Add these to your notes and then make a chart like this.

Uses of oil	Oil companies	Badges
Petrol	Shell	Shell

Talking

Imagine that the steam train and the 125 could speak. What would they say to each other?

Going further

Collect pictures of goods being carried by road, rail and pipeline. Make a list of the things that are carried in more than one way. In these pictures petrol is carried by pipeline, road and rail. Cars are carried by road and rail. Can you find any more?

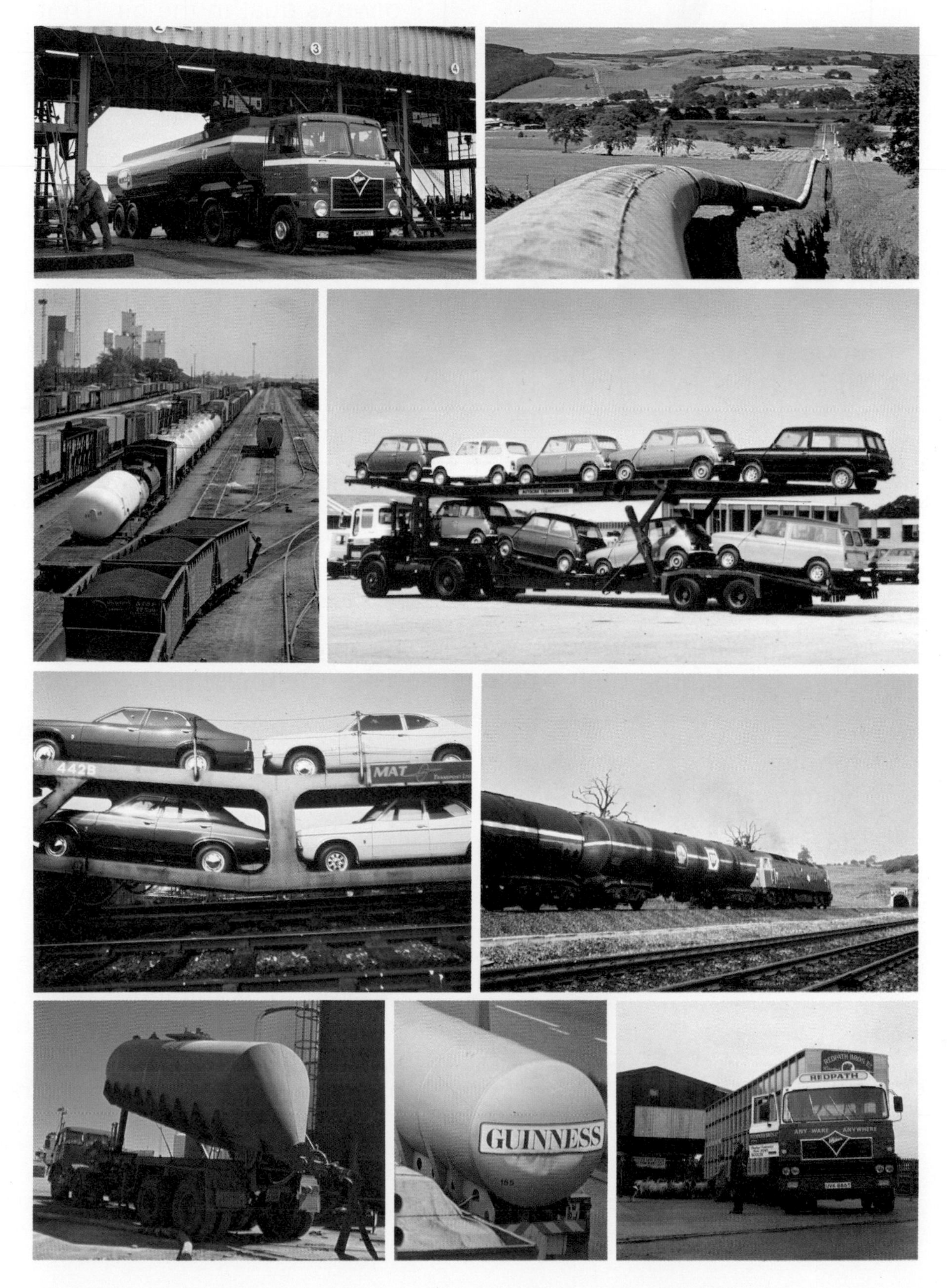

Coal

Robbie is talking to Stan, a miner. He is trying to find out what it is like to be a miner.

Robbie: Is your job dangerous?

Stan: It could be. We have to be very careful. Nobody is allowed to smoke in the mine in case there is some gas there. A lighted match would set off an explosion.

Robbie: Why do you wear a helmet?

Stan: The roof of the mine is sometimes low. I would hurt myself if I hit my head on the roof. The light on the helmet shows the way. It works from a battery I carry with me.

Robbie: Is it very dirty in the mine?

Stan: It is not too bad. It used to be worse. There is always dust in the air. That is why we have big fans underground. They blow fresh air into the mine and help to suck out the dust.

Robbie: My dad told me that miners dig the coal out with shovels.

Stan: No, they don't do that any more. In most mines we don't touch the coal. All the heavy work of digging it out is done by machines.

Robbie: Is it very dark in the mine?

Stan: No, we have electric lights.

Robbie: What is that big wheel behind you?

Stan: We call it the winding gear. A steel rope winds round the wheel. At the end of it is a cage. When we go to work in the mine we get into the cage. The wheel turns and lowers us down the mine.

Do you think mining is an interesting job? Make a list of questions you would ask a miner to find out about his job.

The miner

This week Stan is on the first shift. What time does he start work? Most of us are still asleep at this time. In winter it would still be dark when Stan leaves home. What time does he finish? How many hours does he work in a day?

Stan drives to work in his car. At his mine there are 150 miners. It is a small mine. They work in three shifts so there are fifty miners on each shift.

Thirty of the men go to work in cars. Some drive on their own. Some drive with their friends. The rest get to work on special buses.

When the miners arrive at work they have to clock in like the steelworkers. Then they get ready to go underground. Each man has a locker. He keeps his working clothes in it.

As soon as they are ready the men get in the cage. It is looked after by a lift man who checks everyone in. He rings a bell. This is a signal to another man. He is in the winding house. He releases the brake on the big wheel. This slowly turns and lowers the cage down the shaft on the end of a strong, steel rope.

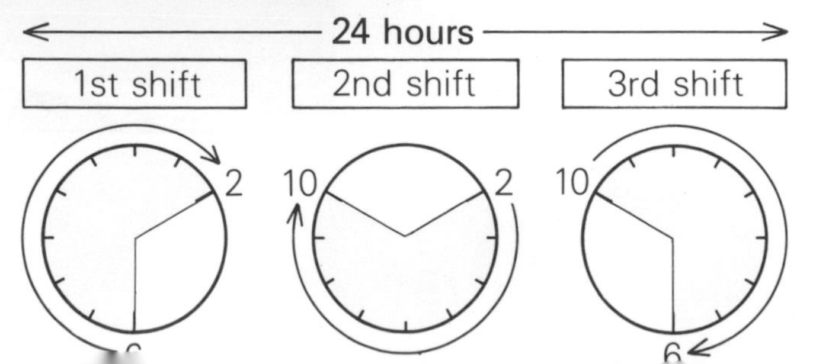

Changes

Coal mines are sometimes called pits. Part of Stan's pit is an old one. It was opened fifty years ago. There are three ways you can tell the old part of the pit. Look at the three pictures. They show what it was like in coal mines fifty years ago. Look at the pictures of the modern mine on page 77. Make a list of things that have changed.

In a few mines the miners themselves still dig out the coal. They often use dynamite to make it easier. This is very carefully packed into holes that the miners have drilled in the rock. When everyone is at a safe distance the dynamite is exploded. It shatters the rock. It is then left for a while. When the dust settles the miners begin loading the coal into waggons. Sometimes they have to break up big lumps. They use picks. It is very hard work.

In a modern pit most of the work is done by machines. Look back at the pictures on page 76. Write down which jobs could be done by machine. The coal-cutting machine can dig out coal. Steel blades cut into the coal and loosen it. Imagine you are underground in a pit. What sort of noises would the coal-cutting machine make? Would they be pleasant?

How many words can you find to describe these noises? Here are some. They have been jumbled up. Sort them out and make the list up to ten.

lcnga	cl---
mpbu	bu--
tosnr	sn-r-
nidgr	--in-
ombo	b---
gbna	---g
spar	-as-

When the coal has been dug by the machine it is loaded on to a moving belt. This is called a conveyor belt. It takes the coal to the top of the pit. Above ground the coal is washed. This gets rid of the dust. It is then sent down chutes into railway waggons. The coal is not touched by hand from the time it is dug out of the rock to the time it is loaded on the waggons.

From mine to home

Look at the picture

It shows two ways of using coal. Follow each path of arrows from the coal mine. When you come to a number or a letter, check the list of labels. Put the correct label next to each number or letter. They have been mixed up in the list.

Old houses
Radiator
Coal merchant
Railway line
Power station
Coal fire
Lorry
Electricity power line
Modern house

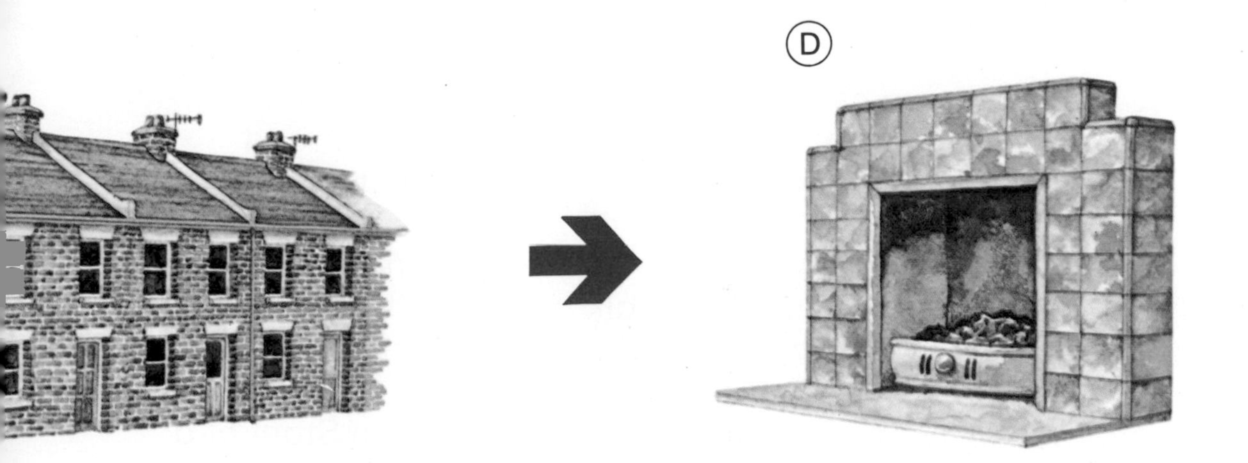

Checking

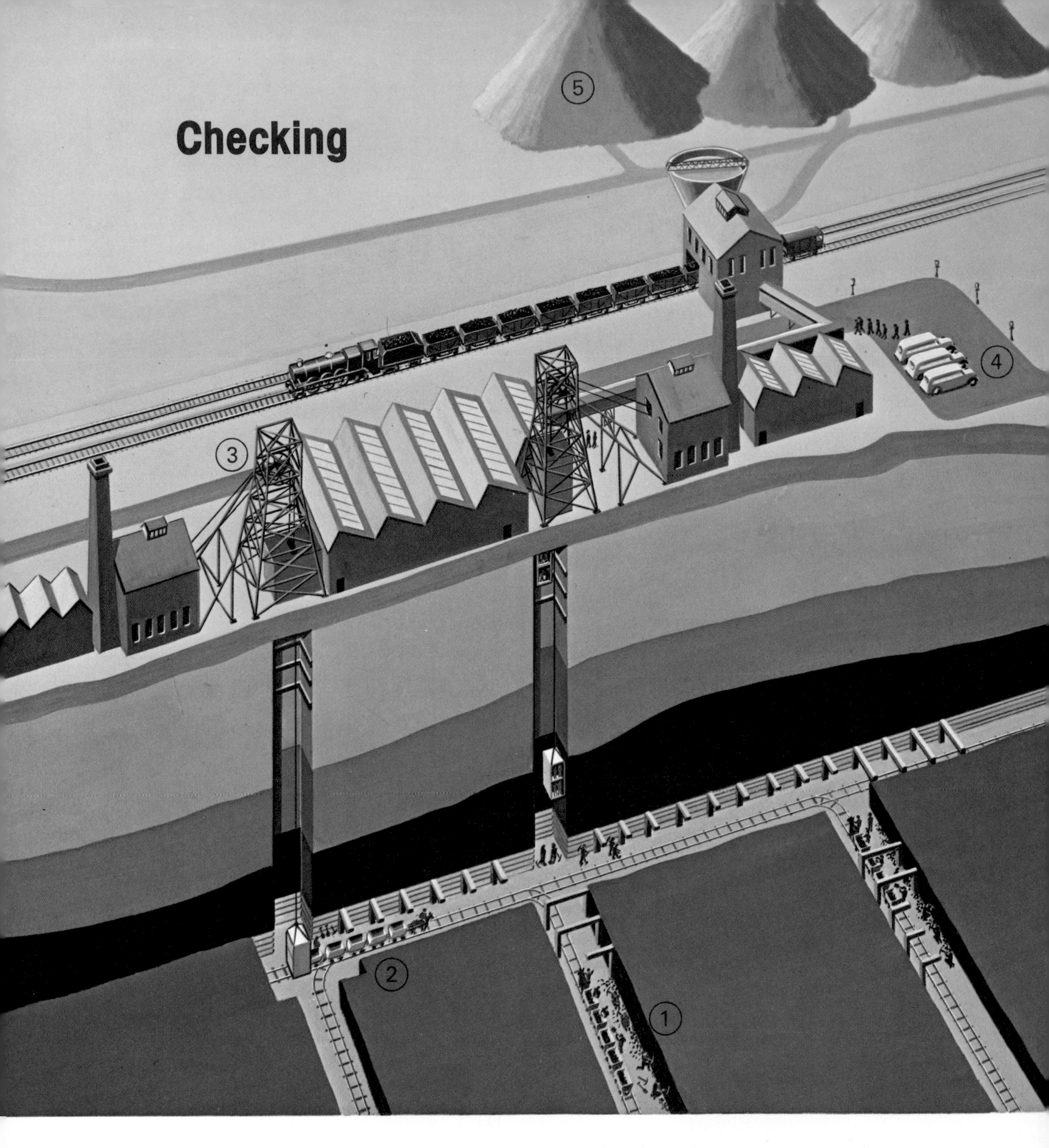

Look at these pictures of a coal mine. They have been drawn so that you can see what is happening underground. On the left you can see how the mine would have looked fifty years ago. On the right is the modern mine.

In the picture are numbers. Make a list of them and next to each, write some sentences to say what is happening in the mine. Talk with your friend about what it is like to be a miner. Use the pictures in this unit to write your own **Story of a piece of coal.**

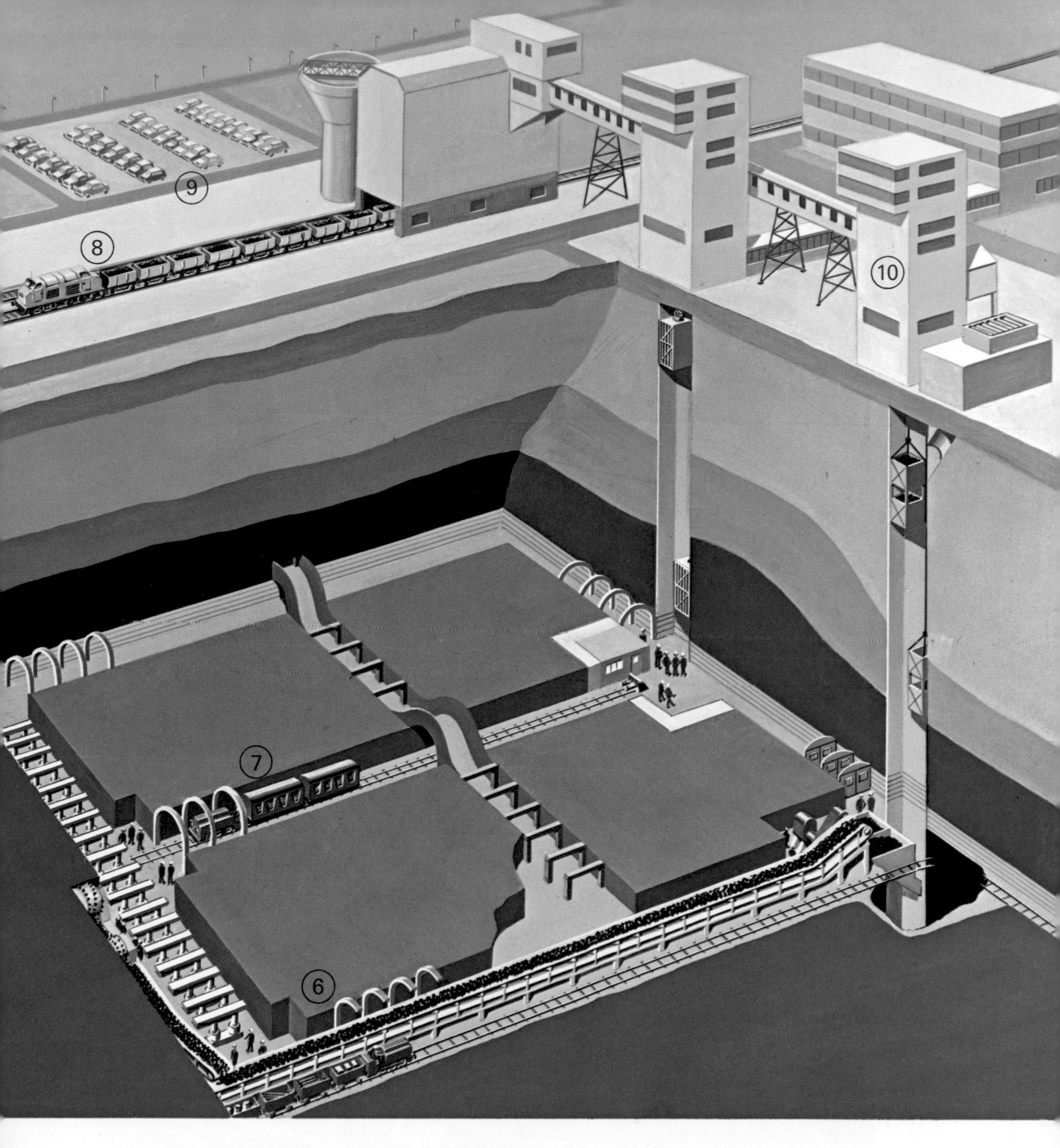

These are five pictures of things a miner wears or uses. Make copies of the pictures and say what each one shows.

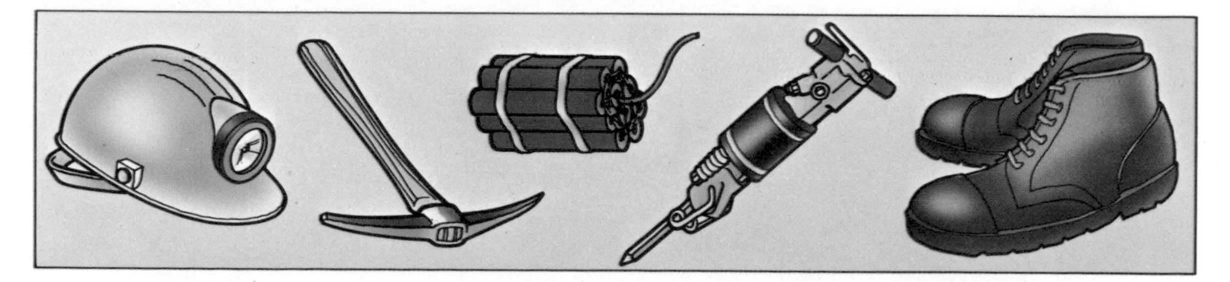

Mountains

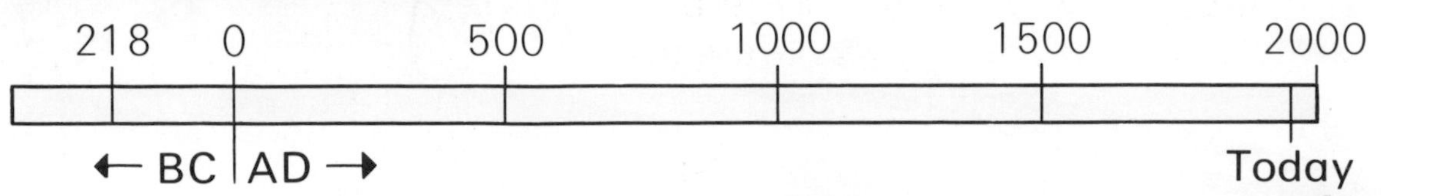

This scene is taking place in 218 BC.

People have gathered in the city of Rome.

News has just arrived. They are in danger of attack. A general called Hannibal has gathered an army in the city of Carthage. He plans to attack the Romans.

Preparing the defences

Imagine you are in charge of the Roman army. You have to prepare to stop the attack.

First decide where the attack will come from.

Look at the map. Which route, **1** or **2**, would Hannibal's soldiers take? How would they get to Rome from Carthage?

Look at the three pictures. They show three ways the Romans could stop an attack. Write down the one you would choose. Then give a reason why. Would you make any other plans to stop the enemy? What would they be?

Build a strong navy so that it could defeat the enemy's fleet before their army could land.

Build strong defences along the coast so the army could not advance.

Make the walls of the city very strong.

Barriers

Hannibal was a clever general. He took his army from Carthage and led it over the Alps to Rome. Look back at the map and follow the way he went. It is shown by a **2**. The Romans had expected him to attack from the sea. So he took them by surprise.

Imagine you are one of Hannibal's soldiers. Look at the four pictures. Each shows a problem you might meet as you are crossing the Alps.

In the first picture an old bridge has been swept away by floods. The river is too deep to cross on foot and therefore forms a barrier. A barrier is something that blocks the way.

Write answers to these questions.

1 What could you do?
2 How would you solve the other three problems?
3 Why did Hannibal think some rivers were a barrier?
4 Why did the Romans think the Alps were a barrier?

The Alps are very high mountains. The highest parts are covered by snow all the year round. In between the mountains are valleys. Valleys are narrow. They have steep sides. The rivers in the valleys often rush down in floods.

The weather can be very bad. Sudden storms break out. It is often cold and there are frequent snow storms.

How many of these things can you see in the picture below? Write about them.

Look at the pictures on page 84. What did Hannibal use elephants for in his army? Can you think of any other way they could be used?

Look at this picture. Write a sentence beginning **Elephants would find it very difficult to cross the Alps because . . .**

The Alps today
0
1
2 km
Mont Rouge
2176m
Buvie
R. Tarn
Tunnel
Highest land
High land
Low land
Mountain peak
River
Road
Bridge
Cable car

Fill in the gaps

Copy out the sentences below. Use the picture and map to find the missing words.

This is part of the Alps. There is a high mountain. It is called ______. It is ______ metres high. Its top is covered in ______. This shows it must be very ______. There are some people ______ on the snow. There is a river. It is called the river ______. A ______ is taking some people up the mountain.

What clues can you find in the picture below which would tell you that you are in a foreign country? Make a list of them.

True or false

Make a copy of the ten sentences below. Then look at the picture on page 86. Now put a ✓ next to the sentences that are true. Put a ✗ next to the false ones.

The first one has been done for you.

1. The sky is blue and there are clouds. ✓
2. There is a lot of snow.
3. There are large stones in the river.
4. The cable car is very high above the valley.
5. There are a lot of lorries on the road.
6. There are many bends in the road.
7. There is a bridge over the river.
8. The mountains are steep.
9. It would be difficult to drive a car on these roads.
10. There is a customs post.

Checking

Spotting shapes

These are some road signs you might see in the Alps. The picture on each one gives you a clue to what the sign means. Draw each one and label it by putting what you think it means. Choose your answer from this list:

dangerous bend
customs
danger from falling rocks
dangerous hill
camping site
beware of animals

The weather

Look back through the unit. Copy down the sentences that tell you about the weather in the Alps. Then sort them into two groups: good weather and bad weather. Make a chart using these headings.

Good weather	Bad weather

Put your sentences into the correct column.

Look at all the pictures to find information about the weather in the Alps. Write some sentences about it.

Other mountains

Turn back to page 32. Copy down what it says about the weather in the Rocky Mountains and on Mount Snowdon.

Find the names of mountains in Scotland, England, South America and North America.

In what kind of book would you find your answers?

What is the highest mountain in the world? Who were the first two people to reach the top?

Clearing snow

This machine is used for clearing snow. Why would it be useful in the mountains? Write some sentences saying how you think it works. Find other ways people fight against bad weather in the mountains.

Mountain passes

When people cross mountains they choose the easiest way. They cross at the lowest part if possible. This is called a mountain pass.

Find the pass in the picture opposite.

Puzzle corner

Mountain passes are often given names. The picture opposite gives you a clue to the name of one in the Alps. What is it?

Try drawing puzzle pictures for these:

Kicking Horse Pass
Crow's Nest Pass
Butter Tubs Pass
Snake Pass

Why did the Italian snowman stop at the mountain cafe?

To have a lunch (avalanche).

Water

These four pictures all show the same thing, or do they? Why has picture **3** been included?

Puzzle corner

Has water any colour?
Look at it to find out.
Can you see through it?
Look at it to find out.
Has it any smell?
Smell it to find out.
Has it any taste?
Sip it to find out.

Why do we say:

as blue as the ocean,
as salty as seawater,
as murky as the deep,
as dull as ditchwater?

Is all water the same?

Finding out

Some days when you go to school it is raining. There are usually dark grey clouds in the sky. The rain is falling from the clouds.

On other days there are no clouds. The sun shines in a clear sky.

When it rains you can see the water. It runs off the roofs. It dances on the playground. It streams down the windows. It collects in puddles.

It is not raining outside this room. But there is a pool of water at the bottom of the window. This is because there is water in the air, even though you cannot see it. When the air touches the glass, it cools. It forms tiny drops of water which cover the window. They are so close together you cannot see outside. After a while the drops slowly slide down the window. They often form a small pool of water on the window sill. Check this on a window in school or at home.

Now write the answers to these questions.

Why do we say the windows are steamed up?

What does the window feel like when you touch it, hot or cold?

Does this give you a clue to why it gets steamed up?

Where do the little pools of water on the window sills come from?

Puzzle corner

These three pictures show a plant, an animal and a car. What are the names of the plant and the animal? Both live in deserts where there is not much water. They stay alive because they can store water. Why does a car need water? Remember a car engine gets very hot when it is running.

Tracing it back

Water flows from the tap.

Water is stored in a tank called a cistern.

A valve is used to stop water flowing.

Some careless person has left the tap on. Drip, drip, drip, drip . . . . Tens, hundreds, thousands of us are escaping. We all stay together. We follow the same track. We form a trickle . . . then a stream . . . over the edge of the sink . . . cascading down the side like a waterfall . . . gathering together on the floor . . . to form a pool.

A house gets its water from big pipes under the street.

These pipes bring water to the town from the reservoir.

This is a lake or reservoir.

Write a story **How the water gets to the home.** Use the pictures to help you.

Here are some words you could use: tap, pipe, cistern, valve, inspection cover, underground pipe, reservoir, concrete dam, lake, deep valley.

This dam was built to block the valley. A lake was formed.

A valve is fixed in a water pipe. It can be turned on and off. When it is **on** the water flows along the pipe because the valve is open. When it is **off** the water stops because the valve is closed and blocks the pipe.

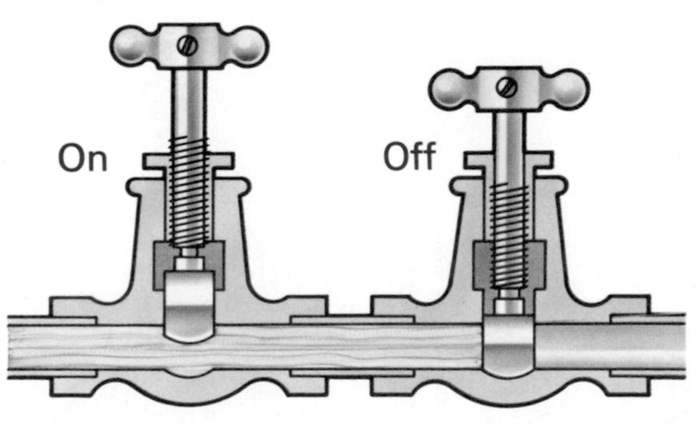

This is a valve.

When pipes run underground there is usually a steel cover over a hole in the ground. The cover can be lifted up. It can be used by the man who checks the pipes.

This is an inspection cover.

Checking

Thinking

How many of the words on page 93 did you know? How many did you find out about? Here are some of the words from page 93. The meanings have been mixed up. Sort them out and copy down the sentences correctly.

1 A **reservoir** is fixed inside a water pipe. It can be turned on and off. It controls the flow of water.

2 An **inspection cover** is built across a valley to make a reservoir.

3 When you did eye-spy in unit 1 did you find a **valve?** They are found on pavements. They can be lifted up to check the water pipes are working properly.

4 A **dam** is a lake where water is stored.

Doing

The picture on page 94 shows a river. It flows into the sea. Before it gets there it goes through forests, past factories, coal mines and towns.

Make a copy of the labels. Look at the picture on page 94. Pick a number from the picture and put it next to its label. We have done **1** and **2** for you. Now try the others.

This is a town.
There are large forests.
This is a coal mine.
It is raining in the hills. **1**
You could go fishing here.
It is a long reservoir. **2**
There is a large factory.
This is where two rivers join.
The river is polluted here.
This flows into the main river.
This part of the river might have coal dust in it.

Some watery jokes

Puzzle corner

These are close-ups of parts of the picture on page 94. Try to see where they fit into the picture.

Synopsis

Oxford New Geography is a complete four-book course for juniors. It introduces the basic skills and concepts of the New Geography at the primary level. The four books are each divided into three sections.

Explorations
How do I find out? How do I record? These and other basic questions are used to develop skills needed by children for a purposeful exploration of the environment. By the use of actual situations children are shown how to look around classroom, school, houses, streets, parks, etc. Familiar situations are used as a springboard for the exploration of less familiar and distant environments.

Face to Face
The emphasis is on presenting lively accounts of people in key occupations as a means of studying the world of work and leisure. Case studies of farms, factories, life in cities and the countryside are used. Children are encouraged to draw comparisons and contrasts with the world they know both at home and abroad.

Links
How are things related and interdependent? From the story of how we get our daily milk and mail to the world of commuters and motorways, the series traces the links that make modern life possible.

The sections contain an average of four units. The units are organized in double-page spreads enabling full use to be made of colour illustrations. The last spread in each unit is used for checking over the work and suggesting lines of further development. Exercises, games and activities cover a wide range of basic geographical skills and concepts.

The Publisher would like to thank the following for permission to reproduce photographs:

Barnaby's Picture Library, pp 16 (centre left), 18, 19 (top left), 25 (right), 68, 69, 73, 89 (top); British Gas, p 67; British Leyland, p 91 (bottom right); British Petroleum, p 73 (top right); British Railways Board, pp 71 (top), 73; Romano Cagnoni, p 49 (bottom right); Bruce Coleman, pp 49 (top right), 89 (bottom), 91 (top right); Colorsport, p 49 (bottom left); Controller of Her Majesty's Stationery Office, p 88; Daily Telegraph Colour Library, pp 32, 71 (bottom), 73; Robert Estall, pp 33 (top), 41 (left); Fodens Ltd, p 73 (top left); Greater London Council, p 63; Susan Griggs, p 73; Kellogg Company of Great Britain Ltd, p 23; Lansing Ltd, p 52; Liverpool City Libraries, p 12 (bottom right); The Mansell Collection Ltd., p 11; David Mellor, p 41 (top left); Merseyside Tramway Preservation Society, p 12 (top right); Oxford County Libraries, pp 12 (left), 13 (top); PAAT, Oxford, pp 9, 22 (top left), 29, 40, 41 (top right, centre right, bottom right), 60, 61, 64, 91 (left), 92, 93; Michael Poulton, p 16 (top left); Redpath Dorman Long & the Cleveland Bridge & Engineering Co Ltd, p 46 (top); Shell UK Oil Ltd, p 72; Spectrum, pp 32, 33 (bottom), 46 (bottom), 91 (centre right); Simon Stafford, pp 13 (bottom), 16 (top right, bottom right), 19 (bottom left), 22 (bottom), 25 (left); Jeffrey Tabberner, p 16 (centre right); Varig Airlines, p 49 (top left); George Wimpey & Co Ltd/Furnas Dam, Brazil, p 46 (centre); Trevor Wood, pp 16 (bottom left), 19 (centre left, right), 22 (top right).

Illustrated by Chris Baker, David Hunt, Ivan Lapper, Edward McLachlan, Miller, Craig & Cocking, Anne Morrow, Graham Smith, Simon Stafford, John Way, Michael Whittlesea. Cover illustration by Ronald Maddox.

Picture Research by Ann Usborne
Design by Stafford & Stafford, Oxford

Book 1

Book 3

Book 4

First published 1980
Reprinted 1981, 1982

Oxford University Press, Walton Street, Oxford OX2 6DP

London Glasgow New York Toronto Delhi Bombay Calcutta Madras Karachi Kuala Lumpur Singapore Hong Kong Tokyo Nairobi Dar es Salaam Cape Town Salisbury Melbourne Auckland

and associate companies in
Beirut Berlin Ibadan Mexico City Nicosia

Filmset by Tradespools Ltd, Frome, Somerset
Printed in Hong Kong

ISBN 0 19 917024 X